Tunisia

Everything You Need to Know

2

Copyright © 2024 by Noah Gil-Smith.

All rights reserved. No part of this book may be reproduced, distributed, or transmitted in any form or by any means, including photocopying, recording, or other electronic or mechanical methods, without the prior written permission of the publisher, except in the case of brief quotations embodied in critical reviews and certain other noncommercial uses permitted by copyright law. This book was created with the assistance of Artificial Intelligence. The content presented in this book is for entertainment purposes only. It should not be considered as a substitute for professional advice or comprehensive research. Readers are encouraged to independently verify any information and consult relevant experts for specific matters. The author and publisher disclaim any liability or responsibility for any loss, injury, or inconvenience caused or alleged to be caused directly or indirectly by the information presented in this book.

Introduction to Tunisia 6

Ancient Tunisia: The Birthplace of Carthage 8

Rise and Fall of Carthage: A Historical Epic 10

The Roman Legacy: Tunisia's Time as Africa Proconsularis 13

The Byzantine Era: Transition and Transformation 15

Islamic Conquest and Arab Influence: Shaping Tunisia's Identity 17

Ottoman Tunisia: The Era of Beydom 20

French Colonialism: Modernization and Struggle 22

Tunisia's Path to Independence: From Protectorate to Republic 25

Modern Tunisia: A Nation in Transition 28

Tunis: Jewel of the Mediterranean 31

Carthage: Ancient Ruins and Modern Charm 33

Sousse: Where History Meets the Sea 36

Sfax: Gateway to the Sahara 38

Djerba: Island of Legends and Traditions 40

Kairouan: The City of a Thousand Mosques 42

Tozeur: Oasis of the South 44

El Jem: Witnessing the Glory of Roman Amphitheaters 46

Dougga: Exploring Tunisia's Best-Preserved Roman City 48

Tunisian Cuisine: A Gastronomic Journey 50

Flavors of Tunisia: From Couscous to Brik 52

Tunisian Delicacies: Sampling Street Food and Sweet Treats 54

Wildlife of Tunisia: From the Atlas Mountains to the Sahara Desert 56

Tunisian Fauna: Discovering the Diverse Wildlife Habitats 59

Desert Treasures: The Flora and Fauna of the Sahara 61

Tunisian Crafts: Artisans and Their Traditions 63

Music and Dance: Rhythms of Tunisian Culture 65

Festivals and Celebrations: Colorful Traditions and Religious Observances 67

Tunisian Architecture: From Ancient Ruins to Modern Marvels 69

Traditional Dress: Exploring Tunisian Clothing Styles 71

Tunisian Literature: Voices of a Nation 73

Tunisian Cinema: A Growing Industry 76

Language and Dialects: Understanding Tunisian Arabic and French 79

The Influence of Berber Languages: Tracing Tunisia's Linguistic Heritage 81

Education in Tunisia: Past, Present, and Future 83

Religion and Society: Islam in Tunisian Life 86

Women's Rights in Tunisia: Progress and Challenges 88

Sports and Recreation: From Football to Camel Racing 91

Economy and Trade: Navigating Tunisia's Business Landscape 94

Tourism in Tunisia: Exploring the Country's Most Iconic Sites 97

Medinas and Souks: Shopping and Sightseeing in Tunisia's Old Towns 100

Beach Resorts: Sun, Sand, and Relaxation on Tunisia's Coastline 102

Adventure Tourism: Exploring Tunisia's Natural Wonders 104

Sustainable Development: Preserving Tunisia's Heritage for Future Generations 106

Epilogue 108

Introduction to Tunisia

Welcome to Tunisia, a land of captivating history, diverse culture, and stunning landscapes nestled along the Mediterranean coast of North Africa. As we embark on this journey, let's delve into the heart of Tunisia, exploring its rich tapestry of civilization, its modern identity, and the myriad wonders that await curious travelers.

Tunisia's story is woven with threads of ancient civilizations dating back thousands of years. One of its most renowned legacies is Carthage, the mighty city-state that rose to prominence in the 9th century BCE. Founded by the Phoenicians, Carthage became a formidable power in the Mediterranean, challenging the might of Rome and leaving an indelible mark on history.

From the ashes of Carthage's destruction emerged the Roman province of Africa Proconsularis, a period marked by prosperity and cultural flourishing. Roman influence can still be seen in Tunisia's archaeological sites, from the majestic amphitheaters of El Jem to the well-preserved ruins of Dougga.

With the spread of Islam in the 7th century CE, Tunisia entered a new era of Arab rule, bringing with it a fusion of cultures and the establishment of great cities such as Kairouan, revered as the fourth holiest city in Islam. The arrival of the Ottomans in the 16th century added another layer to Tunisia's complex identity, as the region became a Beylik under Ottoman suzerainty.

In the 19th century, Tunisia fell under French colonial rule, a period characterized by modernization efforts and growing nationalist sentiment. The struggle for independence culminated in 1956 when Tunisia gained sovereignty, marking the beginning of its modern era as a republic.

Today, Tunisia is a nation in transition, blending its rich heritage with the aspirations of a young population eager to embrace the opportunities of the 21st century. Its capital, Tunis, stands as a vibrant hub of culture and commerce, where ancient medinas and modern skyscrapers coexist in harmony.

Beyond the bustling streets of Tunis lie a wealth of treasures waiting to be discovered. From the ancient ruins of Carthage to the pristine beaches of Djerba, Tunisia offers something for every traveler. Its cuisine, a tantalizing blend of Mediterranean flavors and North African spices, delights the senses, while its diverse landscapes, from the verdant hills of the north to the vast deserts of the south, inspire awe and wonder.

As we delve deeper into the chapters that follow, we will uncover the many facets of Tunisia, from its traditional crafts and vibrant festivals to its thriving film industry and burgeoning tourism sector. Join me as we embark on a journey through this captivating land, where the past meets the present and every corner tells a story waiting to be heard. Welcome to Tunisia.

Ancient Tunisia: The Birthplace of Carthage

In the annals of history, Ancient Tunisia stands as a cradle of civilization, a land where the sands of time whisper tales of greatness and glory. At the heart of this storied land lies Carthage, the legendary city-state that emerged as a beacon of power and influence in the ancient world.

Carthage's origins can be traced back to the 9th century BCE when Phoenician settlers from the city of Tyre embarked on a daring journey across the Mediterranean Sea. Led by Queen Dido, these intrepid explorers sought a new home, a place where they could forge a new destiny amidst the azure waters and fertile lands of North Africa.

Legend has it that Dido, driven by a quest for independence and prosperity, struck a fateful bargain with the local Berber king. As the story goes, she negotiated for as much land as could be encompassed by an oxhide, cleverly cutting the hide into thin strips and encircling a vast territory that would become the foundation of Carthage.

From this humble beginning, Carthage flourished, rising to prominence as a maritime power that rivaled even the mighty city of Rome. Its strategic location along the North African coast enabled Carthage to control vital trade routes, facilitating the exchange of goods and ideas across the Mediterranean.

The Carthaginians were master sailors and traders, venturing far and wide to establish colonies and trading outposts across the Mediterranean basin. These settlements, known as the "Carthaginian Empire," stretched from modern-day Spain and Portugal to Sicily, Sardinia, and beyond, cementing Carthage's status as a dominant force in the ancient world.

Yet, Carthage's prosperity was not without its challenges. The city-state found itself locked in a bitter struggle for supremacy with Rome, a rivalry that would ultimately culminate in a series of devastating conflicts known as the Punic Wars. These wars, fought over control of the western Mediterranean, would shape the course of history and forever alter the destiny of both civilizations.

The most famous figure to emerge from this clash of titans was undoubtedly Hannibal Barca, the Carthaginian general who famously crossed the Alps with his army and waged a relentless campaign against Rome. Despite his tactical brilliance, Hannibal's efforts would ultimately be thwarted, and Carthage would fall to the might of Rome after a long and bloody struggle.

Yet, even in defeat, Carthage left an indelible mark on the world. Its legacy endures in the form of architectural marvels such as the ancient harbor, the Punic Byrsa, and the impressive ruins of the Antonine Baths. The city's influence can also be seen in the spread of its language, culture, and commerce throughout the Mediterranean.

Rise and Fall of Carthage: A Historical Epic

In the annals of history, few tales rival the epic saga of Carthage, a civilization that rose to dizzying heights of power and influence before meeting a tragic end at the hands of its greatest rival, Rome. The rise and fall of Carthage is a story of ambition, innovation, and conflict that echoes through the ages.

The origins of Carthage can be traced back to the Phoenician city-state of Tyre, located in present-day Lebanon. In the 9th century BCE, Tyrian settlers, led by the legendary Queen Dido, established a new colony on the North African coast. This settlement, known as Carthage, would soon become a thriving hub of trade and commerce, its strategic location attracting merchants and sailors from across the Mediterranean.

As Carthage grew in wealth and power, it began to assert its dominance over the western Mediterranean, establishing colonies and trading outposts throughout the region. These colonies, known as the "Carthaginian Empire," stretched from the Iberian Peninsula to Sicily and Sardinia, forming a vast network of maritime influence.

Yet, Carthage's rise to prominence also brought it into conflict with its greatest rival, Rome. The two powers clashed repeatedly over control of the western Mediterranean, culminating in a series of devastating conflicts known as the Punic Wars. These wars, fought over the course of more than a century, would shape the destiny of both civilizations and leave an indelible mark on history.

The first Punic War, which began in 264 BCE, saw Carthage and Rome locked in a bitter struggle for control of Sicily. Despite suffering setbacks at sea, Rome ultimately emerged victorious, seizing Sicily and establishing itself as a major power in the Mediterranean.

The second Punic War, which began in 218 BCE, would see Carthage's most famous general, Hannibal Barca, lead a daring invasion of Italy by crossing the Alps with his army. Hannibal's brilliant tactics and audacious maneuvers won him numerous victories against the Roman legions, including the famous Battle of Cannae in 216 BCE. However, despite his military genius, Hannibal was ultimately unable to deliver a decisive blow to Rome, and the war ended in a stalemate.

The third and final Punic War, which began in 149 BCE, would spell the end for Carthage. Fearing Carthaginian resurgence, Rome launched a full-scale invasion of Carthage, laying siege to the city for three long years. In 146 BCE, Carthage finally fell to the might of Rome, its walls breached, its buildings plundered, and its citizens enslaved or put to the sword.

The destruction of Carthage marked the end of an era and the beginning of Rome's undisputed dominance over the Mediterranean world. Yet, even in defeat, Carthage left a lasting legacy that continues to fascinate and inspire to this day. Its achievements in trade, commerce, and naval technology laid the groundwork for future civilizations, while its tragic demise serves as a cautionary tale of the perils of unchecked ambition and imperial overreach.

The Roman Legacy: Tunisia's Time as Africa Proconsularis

In the annals of Tunisia's history, the Roman legacy stands as a testament to the enduring influence of one of the greatest civilizations the world has ever known. Following the defeat of Carthage in the Punic Wars, Tunisia became a vital part of the Roman Empire, known as Africa Proconsularis.

Under Roman rule, Tunisia experienced a period of unparalleled prosperity and development. The Romans recognized the strategic importance of Tunisia's location, its fertile land, and its abundant natural resources, and they wasted no time in harnessing these assets to their advantage.

One of the most enduring legacies of Roman rule in Tunisia is its impressive network of infrastructure. The Romans built a vast network of roads, bridges, and aqueducts, connecting distant cities and facilitating trade and communication. Many of these structures still stand today, a testament to the engineering prowess of the Roman Empire.

Tunisia's cities flourished under Roman rule, becoming bustling centers of commerce, culture, and governance. The city of Carthage, once the bitter rival of Rome, was rebuilt and transformed into a thriving metropolis, complete with grand public buildings, temples, and theaters.

Other cities, such as Utica, Dougga, and Thuburbo Majus, also thrived during this time, their streets lined with elegant villas, bustling markets, and imposing public monuments. These cities served as important administrative centers, overseeing the governance of the region and serving as hubs of Roman culture and civilization.

One of the most enduring symbols of Roman rule in Tunisia is the amphitheater. These grand arenas, built to host gladiatorial contests, chariot races, and other spectacles, dot the landscape of Tunisia, serving as reminders of the Roman love of entertainment and spectacle.

In addition to its architectural legacy, Roman Tunisia also left its mark on the region's culture and society. Latin became the dominant language of administration and commerce, while Roman law and customs shaped the legal and social systems of the region.

Yet, despite its many achievements, Roman rule in Tunisia was not without its challenges. The region faced periodic unrest and rebellion, as local populations chafed under the yoke of foreign rule. The Romans responded with characteristic ruthlessness, suppressing dissent with force and maintaining control through a combination of military might and political cunning.

Ultimately, the Roman Empire would begin to decline, and Tunisia would find itself caught in the midst of the chaos and upheaval that accompanied its fall. Yet, the legacy of Roman rule would endure, shaping the course of Tunisia's history and leaving an indelible mark on its culture, society, and identity.

The Byzantine Era: Transition and Transformation

In the tapestry of Tunisia's history, the Byzantine Era emerges as a period of transition and transformation, marking a new chapter in the region's rich and diverse cultural landscape. Following the decline of the Roman Empire, Tunisia found itself thrust into a new era of Byzantine rule, as the Eastern Roman Empire sought to assert its authority over the western provinces.

The Byzantine Era in Tunisia began in the 6th century CE, following the conquest of the region by the Byzantine general Belisarius during the reign of the Emperor Justinian I. Under Byzantine rule, Tunisia experienced significant political, social, and religious changes, as the Eastern Empire sought to consolidate its control over the region and integrate it into the wider Byzantine world.

One of the most significant developments of the Byzantine Era was the spread of Christianity throughout Tunisia. The Byzantines, who were staunchly Christian, sought to convert the indigenous population to their faith, establishing churches, monasteries, and religious institutions throughout the region. Many of Tunisia's most iconic Byzantine-era monuments, such as the Basilica of St. Cyprian in Carthage and the Church of St. Vitalis in Sousse, date from this period.

The Byzantine Era also saw significant changes in Tunisia's political and administrative landscape. The Byzantines established a system of provincial governance, dividing the region into smaller administrative units known as dioceses, each overseen by a governor appointed by the imperial authorities. This system helped to centralize power and maintain control over the region's diverse population.

Despite these efforts at centralization, the Byzantine Era was not without its challenges. Tunisia remained a frontier province, vulnerable to incursions from neighboring powers such as the Vandals and the Berber tribes of the interior. These conflicts, combined with internal unrest and periodic rebellions, strained Byzantine resources and tested the empire's ability to maintain control over the region.

The Byzantine Era in Tunisia came to an end in the 7th century CE with the arrival of the Arab Muslim armies during the Islamic conquests. The Byzantines were unable to withstand the onslaught of the Arab forces, and Tunisia fell to Muslim rule after a series of decisive battles. Yet, despite the end of Byzantine rule, the legacy of the Byzantine Era would endure, shaping the cultural, religious, and architectural landscape of Tunisia for centuries to come.

Islamic Conquest and Arab Influence: Shaping Tunisia's Identity

In the colorful tapestry of Tunisia's history, the Islamic conquest and Arab influence emerge as pivotal chapters, shaping the very fabric of the nation's identity. Following the Byzantine Era, Tunisia found itself swept into the transformative tide of Islamic expansion during the 7th century CE. The arrival of Arab Muslim armies brought with it a new religion, language, and culture that would leave an indelible mark on the region.

Islam, a monotheistic faith preached by the Prophet Muhammad, spread rapidly across the Arabian Peninsula and beyond, propelled by the fervor of its followers and the promise of spiritual enlightenment. The Arab conquest of Tunisia was part of this broader movement, as Muslim armies advanced westward, bringing Islam to the shores of North Africa.

The impact of Islam on Tunisia was profound and far-reaching. The arrival of Arab settlers and the conversion of the indigenous population to Islam ushered in a new era of cultural and religious synthesis. The teachings of Islam provided a unifying framework for the diverse peoples of Tunisia, transcending tribal, linguistic, and ethnic divisions.

Under Islamic rule, Tunisia experienced a flowering of intellectual and artistic achievement. Arab scholars and philosophers made important contributions to fields such as mathematics, astronomy, medicine, and literature, laying the groundwork for the European Renaissance and shaping the intellectual landscape of the Muslim world.

Arab influence also left its mark on Tunisia's architecture, cuisine, and social customs. Arab settlers introduced new building techniques, such as the use of mudbrick and decorative tilework, which transformed the region's urban landscape. Arabic became the dominant language of administration, commerce, and culture, supplanting Latin and Byzantine Greek as the lingua franca of Tunisia.

The Islamic conquest of Tunisia also brought with it a new system of governance based on Islamic law, or Sharia. Muslim rulers established dynasties such as the Aghlabids, the Fatimids, and the Zirids, who ruled over Tunisia for centuries, leaving behind a legacy of grand mosques, palaces, and fortifications that still stand as testaments to their power and influence.

Yet, alongside the spread of Islam and Arab culture, Tunisia remained a melting pot of diverse influences, as Berber, Roman, Byzantine, and Phoenician traditions continued to shape the region's identity. The Arab conquest marked the beginning of a process of cultural exchange and hybridization that would continue to evolve over the centuries, enriching Tunisia's cultural heritage and shaping its unique identity as a crossroads of civilizations.

As we reflect on the Islamic conquest and Arab influence, we are reminded of the enduring power of faith, culture, and human connection to shape the course of history. Tunisia's embrace of Islam and Arab culture has left an enduring legacy that continues to shape the nation's identity to this day, forging a sense of unity and belonging that transcends the boundaries of time and space.

Ottoman Tunisia: The Era of Beydom

In the rich tapestry of Tunisia's history, the era of Ottoman rule stands as a pivotal chapter, marked by the rise of the Beydom and the enduring legacy of Ottoman influence. Following the decline of the Hafsid dynasty in the 16th century, Tunisia fell under the control of the Ottoman Empire, which sought to assert its authority over the region and incorporate it into its vast imperial domain.

Under Ottoman rule, Tunisia underwent significant political and social changes. The Ottoman Sultan appointed a governor known as the Bey to oversee the administration of the province, granting him considerable autonomy in exchange for loyalty and tribute. The Bey ruled as the de facto ruler of Tunisia, wielding both political and military power over the region.

The Beydom era saw the consolidation of Ottoman control over Tunisia and the establishment of a system of governance that would endure for centuries. The Bey appointed local officials to administer the provinces, collect taxes, and enforce imperial law, ensuring the stability and security of Ottoman rule.

One of the most enduring legacies of Ottoman rule in Tunisia is the architecture of its cities and towns. The Ottomans brought with them a distinctive architectural style characterized by domed mosques, ornate minarets, and intricately tiled facades. Many of Tunisia's most iconic landmarks, such as the Great Mosque of Kairouan and the Kasbah of Tunis, date from this period.

The Ottomans also left their mark on Tunisia's cultural and religious landscape. Islam, already firmly established in Tunisia, became more deeply intertwined with Ottoman traditions and practices. Sufism, a mystical branch of Islam, flourished under Ottoman patronage, with Sufi orders playing a prominent role in the spiritual and social life of the region.

Economically, Tunisia thrived under Ottoman rule, thanks in part to its strategic location as a gateway between Europe, Africa, and the Middle East. The Ottomans encouraged trade and commerce, investing in the development of ports, markets, and trade routes that linked Tunisia to the wider Ottoman Empire and beyond.

Yet, despite its many achievements, Ottoman rule in Tunisia was not without its challenges. The region faced periodic unrest and rebellion, as local tribes and factions vied for power and influence. The Ottomans responded with a combination of military force and political maneuvering, seeking to maintain control over their restless frontier province.

The era of Ottoman rule in Tunisia would continue until the 19th century, when the region began to experience a decline in Ottoman power and influence. External pressures, such as European imperialism and the rise of nationalist movements, would ultimately contribute to the downfall of Ottoman rule in Tunisia, paving the way for a new chapter in the nation's history.

French Colonialism: Modernization and Struggle

In the annals of Tunisia's history, the chapter of French colonialism stands as a period of profound change, marked by both modernization and struggle. In the 19th century, Tunisia, like many other parts of Africa, found itself caught in the crosshairs of European imperialism as France sought to expand its influence and territories overseas.

The French colonization of Tunisia began in earnest in 1881, when French forces landed on the country's shores and established a protectorate over the region. Under the terms of the Treaty of Bardo, Tunisia effectively became a French colony, with the French Resident-General exercising ultimate authority over the country's affairs.

French colonial rule brought with it a wave of modernization and development. The French introduced new technologies, infrastructure, and administrative systems aimed at modernizing Tunisia and integrating it into the wider French empire. Railways, roads, and ports were built, facilitating the movement of goods and people and opening up new opportunities for trade and commerce.

The French also invested in education and healthcare, establishing schools, hospitals, and universities that laid the groundwork for Tunisia's modernization. French became the language of instruction and administration, and Western-style education became increasingly accessible to Tunisians, albeit primarily to the elite.

Yet, alongside the promises of modernization, French colonialism also brought with it oppression, exploitation, and resistance. The French imposed heavy taxes on the Tunisian population, forcing many peasants into debt and poverty. They also confiscated large swathes of land, displacing countless Tunisians from their ancestral homes and disrupting traditional ways of life.

The Tunisian people, however, did not passively accept French rule. Throughout the colonial period, there were numerous uprisings, protests, and acts of resistance against French oppression. The most notable of these was the Jebel Dyr uprising in 1864, led by the legendary Tunisian freedom fighter, Kharroubi M'barek.

The struggle for independence gained momentum in the 20th century, fueled by the rise of nationalist movements and the desire for self-determination. The Tunisian national movement, led by figures such as Habib Bourguiba and Salah Ben Youssef, called for an end to French colonial rule and the establishment of an independent Tunisian state.

After years of struggle and sacrifice, Tunisia finally gained independence from France in 1956, marking the end of the colonial era and the beginning of a new chapter in the nation's history. French colonialism had left an indelible mark on Tunisia, shaping its identity, its culture, and its path toward modernity. Yet, the legacy of resistance and resilience endured, reminding Tunisians of their enduring spirit and determination to forge their own destiny.

Tunisia's Path to Independence: From Protectorate to Republic

In the turbulent years following World War II, Tunisia embarked on a remarkable journey toward independence, casting off the yoke of colonial rule to reclaim its sovereignty and forge its own destiny as a modern republic. Under French colonialism, Tunisia had been relegated to the status of a protectorate, with the French Resident-General exercising ultimate authority over the country's affairs. However, the winds of change were sweeping across North Africa, and Tunisia's desire for independence grew stronger with each passing day.

The seeds of Tunisia's independence movement were sown in the early 20th century, with the emergence of nationalist leaders such as Habib Bourguiba and Salah Ben Youssef. These charismatic figures galvanized the Tunisian people, calling for an end to French colonial rule and the establishment of a free and sovereign Tunisian state. The movement gained momentum in the wake of World War II, as Tunisians began to agitate for their rights and demand self-determination.

In 1952, Tunisia was rocked by a series of protests and strikes known as the "General Strike," which paralyzed the country and sent shockwaves through the French colonial administration. The French responded with repression and violence, but the Tunisian people remained undeterred, their determination to achieve independence only growing stronger in the face of adversity.

The turning point came in 1954 when Habib Bourguiba and the Neo Destour party launched a campaign of civil disobedience and non-violent resistance against French rule. Their efforts were met with widespread support from the Tunisian population, as well as from the international community, which increasingly viewed colonialism as a relic of the past.

In 1956, the French government finally bowed to pressure and agreed to grant Tunisia its independence. On March 20, 1956, Tunisia officially became a sovereign state, marking the end of over seven decades of French colonial rule. Habib Bourguiba, who had led the independence movement with unwavering determination, became the first President of the Republic of Tunisia.

The years that followed saw Tunisia embark on a journey of nation-building and development, as it sought to chart its own course in the post-colonial world. Bourguiba's government implemented a series of ambitious reforms aimed at modernizing the country and improving the lives of its citizens. These reforms included investments in education, healthcare, and infrastructure, as well as efforts to promote women's rights and social equality.

Tunisia's path to independence was not without its challenges, and the country faced numerous obstacles along the way. Yet, through perseverance, unity, and a steadfast commitment to the ideals of freedom and democracy, Tunisia emerged from the shadows of colonialism to take its place on the world stage as a proud and independent nation.

Modern Tunisia: A Nation in Transition

In the vibrant tapestry of Tunisia's history, the modern era emerges as a period of dynamic change, as the nation navigates the complexities of transition and transformation in the 21st century. Since gaining independence from French colonial rule in 1956, Tunisia has embarked on a journey of nation-building, democracy, and economic development, striving to fulfill the aspirations of its people and secure a brighter future for generations to come.

The early years of independence were marked by optimism and progress, as Tunisia's first president, Habib Bourguiba, implemented a series of ambitious reforms aimed at modernizing the country and improving the lives of its citizens. These reforms included investments in education, healthcare, and infrastructure, as well as efforts to promote women's rights and social equality. Tunisia's economy flourished, driven by a burgeoning tourism industry, a growing manufacturing sector, and a commitment to economic diversification.

However, despite these achievements, Tunisia faced numerous challenges in the decades that followed. Political repression, corruption, and economic inequality undermined the country's progress, fueling discontent and frustration among large segments of the population. In 2011, Tunisia erupted in revolution, as millions of Tunisians took to the streets to demand an end to authoritarian rule and the establishment of a truly democratic government.

The Tunisian Revolution, also known as the Jasmine Revolution, marked a turning point in the nation's history, as it ushered in a new era of democracy and political openness. President Zine El Abidine Ben Ali, who had ruled Tunisia with an iron fist for over two decades, was forced to flee the country, paving the way for free and fair elections and the establishment of a transitional government.

In October 2011, Tunisia held its first democratic elections, which saw the moderate Islamist Ennahda party emerge as the largest political force. The elections were widely hailed as a milestone in Tunisia's transition to democracy, signaling the country's commitment to pluralism, tolerance, and the rule of law.

However, Tunisia's transition to democracy has been far from smooth, as the country grapples with the challenges of political polarization, economic stagnation, and security threats. The assassination of prominent opposition leaders, such as Chokri Belaid and Mohamed Brahmi, underscored the fragility of Tunisia's democratic experiment and the persistence of deep-seated divisions within Tunisian society.

In recent years, Tunisia has made progress in consolidating its democratic institutions and addressing the root causes of social and economic inequality. The adoption of a new constitution in 2014, which enshrines the principles of democracy, human rights, and the rule of law, was a major milestone in Tunisia's transition to democracy. However, significant challenges remain, including the need to combat corruption, strengthen the economy, and address the grievances of marginalized communities.

Despite these challenges, Tunisia remains a beacon of hope and resilience in a region often beset by conflict and instability. Its commitment to democracy, pluralism, and peaceful coexistence serves as an inspiration to people around the world who aspire to freedom and dignity. As Tunisia continues its journey of transition and transformation, it stands poised to realize its full potential as a vibrant and inclusive democracy in the heart of the Arab world.

Tunis: Jewel of the Mediterranean

In the heart of Tunisia lies a city that has captured the imagination of travelers for centuries - Tunis, the Jewel of the Mediterranean. With its rich history, vibrant culture, and stunning architecture, Tunis stands as a testament to the enduring allure of North Africa's coastal gems.

Founded by the Berbers in the 2nd millennium BCE, Tunis has been shaped by a diverse array of influences over the centuries. From the ancient Carthaginians to the Romans, Byzantines, Arabs, and Ottomans, each civilization has left its mark on the city, contributing to its unique blend of cultures, traditions, and architectural styles.

At the heart of Tunis lies the historic Medina, a UNESCO World Heritage Site and one of the best-preserved medieval cities in the world. Here, narrow alleyways wind their way through a labyrinth of souks, mosques, and palaces, offering a glimpse into the city's rich past. The Medina is home to iconic landmarks such as the Zitouna Mosque, the largest mosque in Tunisia, and the stunning Al-Zaytuna University, one of the oldest universities in the Islamic world.

Just outside the Medina lies the modern city center, where bustling boulevards, elegant squares, and majestic buildings reflect Tunis's status as the capital of Tunisia. Here, visitors can explore the Avenue Habib Bourguiba, the city's main thoroughfare, lined with cafes, shops, and cultural institutions. Nearby, the iconic Cathedral of St. Vincent de Paul stands as a testament to Tunisia's multicultural heritage, with its blend of Moorish and European architectural styles.

Beyond its historic and cultural attractions, Tunis is also a city of contrasts, where tradition meets modernity in a dynamic fusion of old and new. In recent years, the city has undergone a period of rapid development, with the construction of modern skyscrapers, shopping malls, and luxury hotels transforming its skyline. Yet, amidst the hustle and bustle of urban life, Tunis has managed to retain its timeless charm and allure, drawing visitors from around the world to its shores.

Tunis is also a city of innovation and creativity, with a thriving arts and cultural scene that reflects its cosmopolitan spirit. From world-class museums and galleries to vibrant street art and music festivals, the city offers a wealth of cultural experiences for visitors to explore and enjoy.

As the gateway to Tunisia's rich cultural heritage and natural beauty, Tunis holds a special place in the hearts of those who visit it. With its warm hospitality, stunning architecture, and vibrant atmosphere, Tunis truly lives up to its reputation as the Jewel of the Mediterranean, beckoning travelers to discover its treasures and secrets for themselves.

Carthage: Ancient Ruins and Modern Charm

Nestled on the coast of Tunisia, overlooking the azure waters of the Mediterranean Sea, lies the ancient city of Carthage – a place where history and modernity converge in a captivating blend of ancient ruins and modern charm. Once a mighty Phoenician stronghold and the capital of a powerful maritime empire, Carthage now stands as a UNESCO World Heritage Site, offering visitors a glimpse into its storied past and vibrant present.

The history of Carthage dates back over 3,000 years, to its founding by Phoenician settlers from Tyre in the 9th century BCE. Over the centuries, Carthage grew into a thriving metropolis, its strategic location making it a hub of trade and commerce in the ancient Mediterranean world. The Carthaginians were renowned sailors and traders, establishing colonies and trading outposts across North Africa, Sicily, and Spain.

Yet, Carthage's rise to power also brought it into conflict with its greatest rival, Rome, leading to a series of devastating wars known as the Punic Wars. Despite the heroic efforts of Carthage's greatest general, Hannibal Barca, the city was ultimately destroyed by the Romans in 146 BCE, its walls torn down, its buildings razed to the ground, and its citizens sold into slavery.

Today, the ruins of ancient Carthage offer a haunting reminder of its former glory, with crumbling walls, shattered columns, and scattered fragments of pottery serving as silent witnesses to its tumultuous past. Visitors to Carthage can explore the remains of its grand public buildings, temples, and theaters, including the famous Baths of Antoninus, the largest Roman baths outside of Rome.

Yet, amidst the ancient ruins, Carthage also exudes a sense of modernity and charm, with its upscale neighborhoods, trendy cafes, and stunning waterfront views. The city's affluent residents and expatriate community lend it an air of sophistication and cosmopolitanism, while its vibrant arts and cultural scene reflects its diverse heritage and identity.

One of the highlights of a visit to Carthage is the Carthage National Museum, which houses a remarkable collection of artifacts and treasures from ancient Carthage, including sculptures, mosaics, and jewelry. The museum offers visitors a fascinating glimpse into the daily life, culture, and achievements of the Carthaginian civilization, helping to bring the city's rich history to life.

Beyond its historical and cultural attractions, Carthage also offers visitors plenty of opportunities for relaxation and recreation, with its picturesque beaches, scenic parks, and bustling markets. The nearby village of Sidi Bou Said, with its whitewashed buildings, cobblestone streets, and breathtaking views, is a popular destination for tourists seeking to escape the hustle and bustle of the city.

As one of the oldest and most storied cities in the world, Carthage continues to captivate and inspire visitors with its ancient ruins and modern charm. Whether exploring its archaeological sites, soaking up its vibrant atmosphere, or simply taking in the stunning views, a visit to Carthage is an experience that will leave a lasting impression on all who journey to its shores.

Sousse: Where History Meets the Sea

Situated along the picturesque coast of Tunisia, Sousse is a city where history seamlessly intertwines with the serene beauty of the sea. With its ancient medina, stunning beaches, and rich cultural heritage, Sousse has long been a beloved destination for travelers seeking to explore the wonders of North Africa.

The history of Sousse stretches back over two millennia, to its founding by the Phoenicians in the 9th century BCE. Over the centuries, the city flourished as a bustling port and trading hub, serving as a gateway between the Mediterranean and the rich interior of Africa. Its strategic location made it a prized possession for successive civilizations, including the Romans, Byzantines, and Arabs, each of whom left their mark on the city's landscape and culture.

Today, Sousse is best known for its stunning medina, a UNESCO World Heritage Site and one of the best-preserved medieval cities in the Arab world. Here, narrow alleyways wind their way through a maze of ancient buildings, souks, and mosques, offering visitors a glimpse into Sousse's rich past. The Great Mosque of Sousse, with its distinctive ribbed dome and towering minaret, stands as a testament to the city's long history of Islamic architecture and craftsmanship.

Beyond its historic medina, Sousse is also home to a wealth of archaeological treasures, including the impressive ruins of the Roman amphitheater, which once hosted gladiatorial contests and other spectacles. Nearby, the Museum of Sousse showcases a fascinating collection of artifacts and relics from Sousse's rich history, including Roman mosaics, Byzantine pottery, and Islamic ceramics.

Yet, perhaps Sousse's greatest attraction lies in its stunning coastline, where miles of sandy beaches stretch out along the azure waters of the Mediterranean Sea. From the bustling resorts of Port El Kantaoui to the secluded coves of Chott Meriem, Sousse offers something for every beach lover, whether it's swimming, sunbathing, or simply enjoying the breathtaking views.

For those seeking a break from the sun and surf, Sousse also boasts a vibrant cultural scene, with art galleries, theaters, and music venues showcasing the talents of local artists and performers. The annual Sousse International Festival, held in the city's historic medina, is a highlight of the cultural calendar, featuring a diverse array of performances, exhibitions, and events that celebrate Sousse's rich heritage and identity.

As the sun sets over the shimmering waters of the Mediterranean, casting a golden glow over Sousse's ancient walls and bustling streets, it's easy to see why this enchanting city has captured the hearts of travelers for centuries. With its blend of history, culture, and natural beauty, Sousse truly offers a glimpse into the soul of Tunisia, where the past meets the present in a harmonious dance of tradition and modernity.

Sfax: Gateway to the Sahara

Nestled on the eastern coast of Tunisia, Sfax stands as a bustling port city and a gateway to the vast expanse of the Sahara Desert. With its rich history, thriving economy, and strategic location, Sfax has long played a central role in the cultural, commercial, and political life of Tunisia.

The history of Sfax dates back over two millennia, to its founding by the Phoenicians in the 9th century BCE. Over the centuries, the city grew into a major center of trade and commerce, serving as a vital link between the Mediterranean and the interior of Africa. Its strategic location made it a coveted prize for successive civilizations, including the Romans, Byzantines, and Arabs, all of whom left their mark on the city's architecture and culture.

Today, Sfax is best known for its bustling port, which ranks as one of the largest and busiest in Tunisia. The port plays a vital role in the country's economy, serving as a hub for trade and shipping, particularly for industries such as textiles, olive oil, and fishing. The port also serves as a gateway for tourists seeking to explore the nearby islands of Kerkennah, with their pristine beaches and charming fishing villages.

In addition to its port, Sfax is also home to a thriving industrial sector, with factories and manufacturing plants producing a wide range of goods, including textiles, ceramics, and processed foods. The city's industrial zone, located on the outskirts of town, is a hive of activity, with thousands of workers employed in factories and warehouses.

Yet, despite its bustling port and industrial sector, Sfax also boasts a rich cultural heritage, with a wealth of historic landmarks and attractions for visitors to explore. The medina of Sfax, with its maze of narrow alleyways and ancient buildings, is a UNESCO World Heritage Site and one of the best-preserved medieval cities in Tunisia. Here, visitors can wander through centuries-old souks, mosques, and madrasas, soaking up the atmosphere of a bygone era.

One of the highlights of a visit to Sfax is the impressive Kasbah, a massive fortress that dominates the city's skyline. Built in the 9th century by the Aghlabid dynasty, the Kasbah served as a military stronghold and administrative center, protecting the city from invaders and providing a refuge for its residents during times of siege.

As the sun sets over the shimmering waters of the Mediterranean, casting a golden glow over Sfax's bustling streets and historic landmarks, it's easy to see why this vibrant city has captured the hearts of travelers for centuries. With its blend of history, industry, and culture, Sfax truly stands as a gateway to the Sahara and a shining jewel in Tunisia's crown.

Djerba: Island of Legends and Traditions

Off the southeastern coast of Tunisia lies the enchanting island of Djerba, a place steeped in legend, tradition, and timeless charm. Known as the "Island of Dreams" to the ancients and immortalized in Homer's Odyssey as the mythical land of the Lotus-Eaters, Djerba has captured the imaginations of travelers for centuries with its pristine beaches, vibrant culture, and rich history.

The history of Djerba dates back thousands of years, to its settlement by Berber tribes in ancient times. Over the centuries, the island has been inhabited by Phoenicians, Romans, Byzantines, Arabs, and Ottomans, each leaving their mark on its landscape and culture. Today, Djerba is home to a diverse population of Arabs, Berbers, and Jews, whose traditions and customs have shaped the island's unique identity.

One of the most iconic landmarks on Djerba is the El Ghriba Synagogue, one of the oldest synagogues in the world and a symbol of the island's rich Jewish heritage. Every year, thousands of pilgrims from around the world gather at the synagogue to celebrate the annual Jewish festival of Lag BaOmer, a testament to the enduring spirit of religious tolerance and coexistence on Djerba.

Djerba is also famous for its stunning beaches, which stretch for miles along the island's coastline, offering visitors the perfect setting for swimming, sunbathing, and water sports. From the popular resort town of Houmt Souk to the secluded beaches of Ras Rmel and Sidi Mahrez, Djerba has something for every beach lover, whether it's relaxation or adventure.

In addition to its natural beauty, Djerba is also known for its vibrant arts and cultural scene, with a wealth of museums, galleries, and festivals showcasing the island's rich heritage and creativity. The Museum of Guellala, housed in a traditional Berber cave dwelling, offers visitors a fascinating glimpse into the island's history and culture, while the International Festival of Djerba, held annually in July, features a diverse array of music, dance, and theater performances from around the world.

For those seeking adventure, Djerba offers plenty of opportunities for exploration, with its ancient ruins, desert oases, and bustling souks. The Roman ruins of Meninx, with their well-preserved mosaics and temples, provide a fascinating glimpse into the island's Roman past, while the desert town of Matmata, famous for its underground troglodyte dwellings, offers a glimpse into traditional Berber life.

As the sun sets over the tranquil waters of the Mediterranean, casting a golden glow over Djerba's whitewashed buildings and palm-fringed beaches, it's easy to see why this enchanting island has captured the hearts of travelers for centuries. With its blend of legend, tradition, and natural beauty, Djerba truly stands as a timeless destination where dreams come to life and memories are made to last a lifetime.

Kairouan: The City of a Thousand Mosques

Nestled in the heart of Tunisia, amid the rolling hills of the Sahel region, lies the ancient city of Kairouan, a place of profound spiritual significance and architectural splendor. Known as the "City of a Thousand Mosques," Kairouan holds a special place in the hearts of Muslims around the world, revered for its rich history, cultural heritage, and breathtaking monuments.

Founded in the 7th century CE by the Umayyad general Uqba ibn Nafi, Kairouan quickly rose to prominence as a center of Islamic learning, trade, and religion. Its strategic location along ancient trade routes made it a hub of commerce and culture, attracting scholars, merchants, and pilgrims from across the Islamic world.

One of the most iconic landmarks in Kairouan is the Great Mosque, also known as the Mosque of Uqba, which stands as one of the oldest and most important mosques in North Africa. Built in the 7th century, the Great Mosque is a masterpiece of Islamic architecture, with its towering minaret, intricate tilework, and serene courtyards drawing visitors from far and wide.

Yet, the Great Mosque is just one of many mosques that dot the cityscape of Kairouan, earning it the nickname "City of a Thousand Mosques." From the elegant domes and minarets of the Mosque of the

Three Doors to the grandeur of the Mosque of the Barber, each mosque in Kairouan tells a story of faith, devotion, and architectural ingenuity.

In addition to its mosques, Kairouan is also home to a wealth of other historic and cultural attractions, including the Aghlabid Basins, a series of reservoirs and cisterns built in the 9th century to supply the city with water. Nearby, the Museum of Islamic Art houses a remarkable collection of artifacts and treasures from Kairouan's illustrious past, including ceramics, textiles, and manuscripts.

For centuries, Kairouan has served as a center of Islamic scholarship and spiritual reflection, attracting scholars, mystics, and pilgrims from across the Muslim world. The city's madrasas, or religious schools, played a central role in the transmission of knowledge and learning, fostering a culture of intellectual inquiry and religious devotion that continues to thrive to this day.

As the sun sets over the ancient walls and winding streets of Kairouan, casting a golden glow over its majestic mosques and tranquil courtyards, it's easy to see why this historic city holds such a special place in the hearts of Muslims around the world. With its rich history, cultural heritage, and spiritual significance, Kairouan truly stands as a testament to the enduring power and beauty of Islamic civilization.

Tozeur: Oasis of the South

Nestled amidst the arid landscapes of southern Tunisia, lies the enchanting oasis town of Tozeur, a hidden gem renowned for its lush palm groves, traditional architecture, and rich cultural heritage. Surrounded by the vast expanse of the Sahara Desert, Tozeur stands as a beacon of life and vitality in an otherwise harsh and unforgiving environment.

The history of Tozeur dates back thousands of years, to its founding by Berber tribes who settled in the region and built the first irrigation systems to cultivate the land. Over the centuries, Tozeur grew into a thriving oasis town, its fertile soil and abundant water attracting settlers, traders, and travelers from across North Africa and beyond.

One of the most striking features of Tozeur is its palm groves, which stretch for miles along the banks of the Oued El Maleh, a seasonal river that flows through the town. These lush green oases provide a stark contrast to the surrounding desert landscape, offering a haven of shade, tranquility, and natural beauty for both locals and visitors alike.

In addition to its palm groves, Tozeur is also known for its distinctive architecture, with its traditional earthen buildings and ornate facades reflecting the town's rich cultural heritage. The old medina of Tozeur, with its narrow alleyways and whitewashed buildings, is a UNESCO World Heritage Site and one of the best-preserved examples of traditional North African architecture in the region.

One of the highlights of a visit to Tozeur is the Chak Wak, a traditional irrigation system that dates back over a thousand years and is still in use today. This ingenious system of underground channels and wells distributes water from the nearby mountains to the palm groves and fields surrounding the town, ensuring the continued prosperity of Tozeur's agricultural economy.

For centuries, Tozeur has been a center of commerce and culture in southern Tunisia, serving as a crossroads for trade between the Mediterranean coast and the interior of Africa. The town's bustling souks, or markets, are a hive of activity, with vendors selling a colorful array of goods, including spices, textiles, and handicrafts.

In recent years, Tozeur has also emerged as a popular tourist destination, attracting visitors from around the world with its unique blend of natural beauty, cultural heritage, and outdoor activities. From camel rides through the desert dunes to excursions to nearby attractions such as the Chebika Oasis and the Star Wars film sets, there is no shortage of things to see and do in Tozeur.

As the sun sets over the palm groves and minarets of Tozeur, casting a warm glow over the town's ancient streets and bustling markets, it's easy to see why this oasis of the south holds such a special place in the hearts of those who visit it. With its timeless beauty, rich history, and warm hospitality, Tozeur truly stands as a testament to the enduring spirit of life in the desert.

El Jem: Witnessing the Glory of Roman Amphitheaters

In the heart of Tunisia, amidst the golden sands and olive groves, stands the ancient city of El Jem, a place where visitors can witness the awe-inspiring glory of Roman amphitheaters. El Jem is home to one of the most impressive and well-preserved Roman amphitheaters in the world, a testament to the architectural prowess and engineering ingenuity of the ancient Romans.

Built in the 3rd century CE during the reign of Emperor Gordian, the Amphitheater of El Jem is a marvel of Roman engineering, with its towering walls, grand arches, and imposing facade. Originally capable of seating up to 35,000 spectators, the amphitheater was used for gladiatorial contests, chariot races, and other spectacles that entertained the citizens of ancient Thysdrus, as El Jem was known in Roman times.

Today, the Amphitheater of El Jem is a UNESCO World Heritage Site and one of the most iconic landmarks in Tunisia, drawing visitors from around the world to marvel at its grandeur and historical significance. Despite centuries of neglect and decay, much of the amphitheater's structure remains intact, allowing visitors to imagine themselves transported back in time to the days of the Roman Empire.

One of the most impressive features of the Amphitheater of El Jem is its underground passages and chambers, which were used to house animals, gladiators, and prisoners before they were brought into the arena. These labyrinthine tunnels provide a fascinating glimpse into the inner workings of the amphitheater and the lives of those who inhabited it.

In addition to its amphitheater, El Jem is also home to a wealth of other historic and cultural attractions, including the Archaeological Museum of El Jem, which houses a remarkable collection of artifacts and relics from the Roman period. Nearby, the ancient ruins of Thysdrus offer visitors the opportunity to explore the remains of a once-thriving Roman city, including temples, baths, and villas.

Beyond its historical and cultural attractions, El Jem also offers visitors the chance to experience the vibrant culture and warm hospitality of modern Tunisia. The town's bustling souks, lively cafes, and traditional restaurants provide ample opportunities to sample local cuisine, shop for handicrafts, and mingle with the friendly locals.

Dougga: Exploring Tunisia's Best-Preserved Roman City

Nestled amidst the rolling hills of northern Tunisia lies Dougga, a hidden gem and one of the best-preserved Roman cities in the country. Stepping foot into Dougga is like stepping back in time, as visitors are transported to the heart of the Roman Empire, where grand temples, imposing theaters, and majestic arches stand as silent witnesses to the city's illustrious past.

Originally founded as a Numidian settlement in the 6th century BCE, Dougga flourished under Roman rule, reaching its peak in the 2nd and 3rd centuries CE. At its height, Dougga was a bustling metropolis, home to thousands of inhabitants and a hub of trade, commerce, and culture in the region.

One of the most impressive features of Dougga is its well-preserved theater, which dates back to the 2nd century CE and is one of the largest and best-preserved Roman theaters in North Africa. With its tiered seating, commanding views of the surrounding countryside, and acoustics that rival those of modern concert halls, the theater is a testament to the architectural prowess and artistic achievements of the ancient Romans.

In addition to its theater, Dougga is also home to a wealth of other historic and cultural attractions, including the Capitol, a grand temple dedicated to the Roman gods Jupiter, Juno, and Minerva. Nearby, the Temple of Saturn, with its towering columns and intricate carvings, offers visitors a glimpse into the religious life of ancient Dougga.

Another highlight of a visit to Dougga is the well-preserved Roman baths, which provide a fascinating insight into the daily life and hygiene practices of the city's inhabitants. Here, visitors can explore the remains of hot and cold baths, steam rooms, and massage chambers, marveling at the ingenuity of Roman engineering and craftsmanship.

Beyond its archaeological wonders, Dougga also offers visitors the chance to experience the natural beauty and tranquility of the Tunisian countryside. Surrounded by lush olive groves and vineyards, with panoramic views of the distant mountains, Dougga is the perfect destination for hiking, picnicking, and exploring the great outdoors.

As the sun sets over the ancient ruins and rolling hills of Dougga, casting a warm glow over its majestic temples and bustling streets, it's easy to see why this hidden gem holds such a special place in the hearts of those who visit it. With its blend of history, culture, and natural beauty, Dougga truly stands as a testament to the enduring legacy of the Roman Empire and the timeless allure of Tunisia.

Tunisian Cuisine: A Gastronomic Journey

Embark on a mouthwatering journey through the diverse and flavorful cuisine of Tunisia, a culinary landscape shaped by centuries of history, culture, and tradition. From aromatic spices to fresh seafood, Tunisian cuisine is a tantalizing blend of Mediterranean, Arab, Berber, and French influences, reflecting the country's rich and diverse culinary heritage.

At the heart of Tunisian cuisine is the humble yet versatile olive, which plays a central role in many dishes, from salads and stews to couscous and pastries. Tunisia is one of the world's largest producers of olives and olive oil, with each region boasting its own unique variety and flavor profile.

One of the most iconic dishes in Tunisian cuisine is couscous, a hearty and flavorful grain dish that is traditionally served with a variety of meats, vegetables, and aromatic spices. Whether enjoyed as a simple weekday meal or as the centerpiece of a festive celebration, couscous is a staple of Tunisian cooking and a true labor of love for many home cooks.

Another beloved Tunisian dish is brik, a crispy pastry filled with a savory mixture of egg, tuna, capers, and parsley, then deep-fried to golden perfection. Brik is a popular street food snack in Tunisia, often enjoyed with a squeeze of lemon juice and a sprinkle of harissa, a fiery chili paste that adds a bold kick of flavor to any dish.

Seafood also features prominently in Tunisian cuisine, thanks to the country's long coastline and rich maritime heritage. From grilled sardines to stuffed squid, Tunisian seafood dishes are known for their fresh flavors and simple preparation, allowing the natural taste of the fish to shine through.

No discussion of Tunisian cuisine would be complete without mentioning harissa, the spicy chili paste that adds heat and depth to many dishes. Made from a blend of dried red chilies, garlic, olive oil, and spices, harissa is a staple condiment in Tunisian kitchens and is often served alongside bread, couscous, and grilled meats.

For those with a sweet tooth, Tunisian cuisine offers a tantalizing array of desserts and pastries, from sticky-sweet baklava to flaky almond-filled pastries known as makroudh. Many Tunisian desserts are made with local ingredients such as dates, almonds, and honey, reflecting the country's rich agricultural heritage and love of all things sweet.

As you journey through the vibrant markets and bustling cafes of Tunisia, you'll discover a world of flavors and aromas that will delight your senses and leave you craving more. Whether sampling street food in the medina, dining in a cozy family-run restaurant, or savoring a leisurely meal overlooking the sea, Tunisian cuisine is sure to leave a lasting impression on your taste buds and your heart.

Flavors of Tunisia: From Couscous to Brik

Embark on a delectable journey through the vibrant and diverse flavors of Tunisia, a culinary tapestry woven with influences from the Mediterranean, Arab, Berber, and French traditions. From the aromatic spices of the souks to the fresh seafood of the coast, Tunisian cuisine is a tantalizing fusion of flavors, textures, and colors that reflect the country's rich history and cultural heritage.

At the heart of Tunisian cuisine lies couscous, a versatile grain dish that serves as a staple in the diet of many Tunisians. Traditionally made from semolina wheat, couscous is steamed to fluffy perfection and served with a variety of meats, vegetables, and aromatic spices. Whether enjoyed as a simple weekday meal or as the centerpiece of a festive celebration, couscous is a true labor of love for many Tunisian home cooks.

Another iconic Tunisian dish is brik, a crispy pastry filled with a savory mixture of egg, tuna, capers, and parsley, then deep-fried to golden perfection. Brik is a popular street food snack in Tunisia, often enjoyed with a squeeze of lemon juice and a dollop of fiery harissa, a spicy chili paste that adds a bold kick of flavor to any dish.

Seafood also features prominently in Tunisian cuisine, thanks to the country's long coastline and rich maritime heritage. From grilled sardines to stuffed squid, Tunisian seafood dishes are known for their fresh flavors and simple preparation, allowing the natural taste of the fish to shine through.

Speaking of harissa, it's worth mentioning that this fiery chili paste is a staple condiment in Tunisian kitchens, adding heat and depth to many dishes. Made from a blend of dried red chilies, garlic, olive oil, and spices, harissa is often served alongside bread, couscous, and grilled meats, adding a fiery kick to every bite.

For those with a sweet tooth, Tunisian cuisine offers a tantalizing array of desserts and pastries, from sticky-sweet baklava to flaky almond-filled pastries known as makroudh. Many Tunisian desserts are made with local ingredients such as dates, almonds, and honey, reflecting the country's rich agricultural heritage and love of all things sweet.

As you explore the bustling markets and lively cafes of Tunisia, you'll discover a world of flavors and aromas that will delight your senses and leave you craving more. Whether sampling street food in the medina, dining in a cozy family-run restaurant, or savoring a leisurely meal overlooking the sea, Tunisian cuisine is sure to leave a lasting impression on your taste buds and your heart.

Tunisian Delicacies: Sampling Street Food and Sweet Treats

In the bustling streets and lively markets of Tunisia, a world of culinary delights awaits those willing to explore. From savory street food to delectable sweet treats, Tunisian cuisine is a vibrant tapestry of flavors, textures, and aromas that reflect the country's rich cultural heritage and diverse culinary traditions.

One of the best ways to experience Tunisian cuisine is by sampling the street food that lines the bustling thoroughfares of cities like Tunis, Sousse, and Sfax. Here, you'll find a tantalizing array of savory snacks and quick bites, from crispy falafel and savory brik to hearty merguez sandwiches and spicy kebabs.

One of the most popular street food dishes in Tunisia is brik, a crispy pastry filled with a savory mixture of egg, tuna, capers, and parsley, then deep-fried to golden perfection. Brik is a favorite among locals and visitors alike, often enjoyed as a quick snack or appetizer on the go.

Another must-try street food in Tunisia is merguez, a spicy lamb or beef sausage that is grilled to perfection and served in a warm baguette with a generous dollop of harissa, a fiery chili paste that adds a bold kick of flavor to every bite. Merguez sandwiches are a staple of Tunisian street food culture and are sure to leave you craving more.

For those with a sweet tooth, Tunisian street food offers a tantalizing array of desserts and pastries that are sure to satisfy even the most discerning palates. From sticky-sweet baklava to flaky almond-filled pastries known as makroudh, there's no shortage of indulgent treats to tempt your taste buds.

In addition to street food, Tunisian cuisine also boasts a rich tradition of sweet treats and desserts that are enjoyed during special occasions and celebrations. One of the most beloved Tunisian desserts is mahalabiya, a creamy pudding made from milk, sugar, and rosewater, then topped with chopped pistachios or almonds for added crunch and flavor.

Another popular Tunisian sweet treat is kaak warka, a delicate pastry made from layers of thin dough that are rolled out, stuffed with a sweet almond paste, and then baked until golden brown and crispy. Kaak warka is often enjoyed during the holy month of Ramadan and other festive occasions, where it is served alongside mint tea as a symbol of hospitality and celebration.

As you wander the vibrant streets and alleys of Tunisia, be sure to indulge in the rich tapestry of flavors and aromas that await you at every turn. From savory street food to decadent desserts, Tunisian cuisine is sure to leave you craving more and eager to explore all that this culinary paradise has to offer.

Wildlife of Tunisia: From the Atlas Mountains to the Sahara Desert

Welcome to the wild side of Tunisia, where a diverse array of landscapes provides habitats for an impressive variety of wildlife, from the rugged peaks of the Atlas Mountains to the vast expanse of the Sahara Desert. Despite its relatively small size, Tunisia boasts a rich biodiversity, with species adapted to its varied terrain and climate.

Let's start with the Atlas Mountains, a rugged range that stretches across northern Tunisia. Here, in the mountainous regions, you'll find a wealth of flora and fauna, including the Barbary macaque, North Africa's only primate species. These charismatic monkeys roam the forested slopes of the Atlas Mountains, foraging for food and entertaining visitors with their playful antics.

In addition to the Barbary macaque, the Atlas Mountains are also home to a variety of bird species, including eagles, hawks, and vultures. These birds of prey soar high above the mountain peaks, scanning the landscape for prey and playing a crucial role in maintaining the delicate balance of the ecosystem.

As we venture southward into the Sahara Desert, the landscape changes dramatically, giving way to vast expanses of sand dunes, rocky plateaus, and dry riverbeds. Despite its harsh and unforgiving environment, the Sahara is home to a surprising variety of wildlife, adapted to life in one of the most extreme environments on Earth.

One of the most iconic inhabitants of the Sahara Desert is the dromedary camel, also known as the Arabian camel. These hardy animals are well adapted to life in the desert, with their long legs, thick fur, and specialized nostrils that allow them to survive in the harsh desert climate. Dromedary camels have been used for centuries by the nomadic Berber tribes of the Sahara, providing transportation, food, and shelter for those who call this harsh environment home.

In addition to camels, the Sahara Desert is also home to a variety of reptiles, including desert monitors, sand vipers, and desert tortoises. These cold-blooded creatures have evolved a range of adaptations to help them survive in the desert, from their ability to burrow underground to their specialized scales and camouflage patterns.

Of course, no discussion of the wildlife of Tunisia would be complete without mentioning the country's rich marine biodiversity. The Mediterranean Sea, which borders Tunisia to the north, is home to a variety of fish, crustaceans, and marine mammals, including dolphins, swordfish, and octopuses. The waters around Tunisia are also home to several species of sea turtles, including the endangered loggerhead turtle, which nests on the country's beaches during the summer months.

From the mountains to the desert to the sea, Tunisia's diverse landscapes provide habitats for an incredible variety of wildlife, each adapted to its own unique environment. Whether you're exploring the forests of the Atlas Mountains, trekking across the dunes of the Sahara Desert, or diving into the crystal-clear waters of the Mediterranean Sea, you're sure to encounter a fascinating array of creatures that call Tunisia home.

Tunisian Fauna: Discovering the Diverse Wildlife Habitats

Welcome to the fascinating world of Tunisian fauna, where a rich tapestry of ecosystems provides habitats for an incredible diversity of wildlife. From the dense forests of the Atlas Mountains to the vast expanse of the Sahara Desert, Tunisia is home to a wide range of species adapted to its varied terrain and climate.

Let's begin our journey in the northern regions of Tunisia, where the Atlas Mountains rise majestically above the landscape. Here, in the cool and forested slopes of the mountains, you'll find an abundance of flora and fauna, including the Barbary macaque, North Africa's only primate species. These charismatic monkeys roam freely in the cedar and oak forests, foraging for food and entertaining visitors with their playful antics.

As we venture southward into the arid plains and rocky plateaus of central Tunisia, the landscape becomes increasingly harsh and unforgiving. Despite the challenging conditions, a surprising variety of wildlife thrives in this desert environment, adapted to life in one of the most extreme climates on Earth.

One of the most iconic inhabitants of the Tunisian desert is the dromedary camel, also known as the Arabian camel. These hardy animals are well adapted to the desert environment, with their long legs, thick fur, and specialized nostrils that allow them to survive in the harsh conditions of the Sahara. Dromedary camels have been used for centuries by the nomadic Berber tribes of the desert, providing transportation, food, and shelter for those who call this arid landscape home.

In addition to camels, the Sahara Desert is also home to a variety of reptiles, including desert monitors, sand vipers, and desert tortoises. These cold-blooded creatures have evolved a range of adaptations to help them survive in the harsh desert environment, from their ability to burrow underground to their specialized scales and camouflage patterns.

Of course, no discussion of Tunisian fauna would be complete without mentioning the country's rich marine biodiversity. The Mediterranean Sea, which borders Tunisia to the north, is teeming with life, from colorful coral reefs to majestic marine mammals. Dolphins, swordfish, and octopuses are just a few of the species that call these waters home, while endangered loggerhead turtles nest on Tunisia's beaches during the summer months.

Whether you're exploring the forests of the Atlas Mountains, trekking across the dunes of the Sahara Desert, or diving into the crystal-clear waters of the Mediterranean Sea, Tunisia's diverse habitats offer endless opportunities to discover and marvel at the incredible diversity of its wildlife.

Desert Treasures: The Flora and Fauna of the Sahara

Welcome to the Sahara Desert, a vast and seemingly inhospitable landscape that is home to a surprising variety of flora and fauna, each uniquely adapted to life in one of the harshest environments on Earth. Despite its extreme conditions, the Sahara is teeming with life, from hardy desert plants to elusive desert-dwelling animals.

Let's start with the flora of the Sahara, where a variety of plant species have evolved ingenious adaptations to survive in the desert environment. One of the most iconic desert plants is the date palm, which thrives in the oases scattered throughout the Sahara, providing shade, sustenance, and shelter for both humans and wildlife alike. The date palm's ability to withstand drought and extreme temperatures makes it a vital resource for desert communities and a symbol of resilience in the face of adversity.

In addition to date palms, the Sahara is also home to a variety of other plant species, including acacia trees, tamarisks, and succulent plants such as cacti and agave. These plants have developed a range of adaptations to help them survive in the harsh desert climate, from deep root systems that tap into underground water sources to waxy coatings that reduce water loss through evaporation.

Turning our attention to the fauna of the Sahara, we encounter a diverse array of animals that have evolved remarkable adaptations to thrive in this challenging environment. One of the most iconic desert animals is the dromedary camel, also known as the Arabian camel, which has been domesticated for thousands of years by the nomadic peoples of the Sahara. With their long legs, thick fur, and specialized nostrils, dromedary camels are perfectly suited to life in the desert, able to endure extreme temperatures and go for long periods without water.

In addition to camels, the Sahara is also home to a variety of other desert-dwelling animals, including desert foxes, sand cats, and fennec foxes. These elusive creatures have evolved a range of adaptations to help them survive in the harsh desert environment, from their ability to burrow underground to their keen senses of hearing and smell.

Birds also play a crucial role in the Sahara ecosystem, with species such as ostriches, desert sparrows, and raptors thriving in the desert environment. Many of these birds are migratory, traveling vast distances across the Sahara in search of food and water, and playing a vital role in maintaining the delicate balance of the ecosystem.

As you journey through the Sahara Desert, you'll discover a world of hidden treasures waiting to be explored, from the towering sand dunes to the rocky plateaus and ancient oases. Whether you're marveling at the resilience of desert plants, tracking elusive desert animals, or simply soaking in the awe-inspiring beauty of the desert landscape, the Sahara is sure to leave a lasting impression on your heart and soul.

Tunisian Crafts: Artisans and Their Traditions

In the colorful tapestry of Tunisian culture, artisan crafts hold a cherished place, weaving together tradition, skill, and creativity into exquisite works of art. From the bustling souks of Tunis to the quiet workshops of rural villages, artisans across Tunisia carry on centuries-old traditions, passing down their skills and knowledge from generation to generation.

One of the most iconic Tunisian crafts is pottery, with artisans in cities like Nabeul and Sejnane creating beautiful ceramics adorned with intricate patterns and vibrant colors. Using techniques handed down through the ages, these skilled craftsmen mold and shape clay into a variety of forms, from decorative vases and bowls to functional kitchenware and tiles. Each piece is a testament to the artisan's skill and creativity, reflecting the rich cultural heritage of Tunisia.

Another revered Tunisian craft is carpet weaving, with artisans in regions such as Kairouan and El Kef producing stunning rugs and carpets using traditional techniques passed down through the centuries. Using locally-sourced wool and natural dyes, these skilled weavers create intricate designs and patterns that tell stories of Tunisian history, culture, and identity. Each carpet is a labor of love, with some taking months or even years to complete, showcasing the artisan's dedication and craftsmanship.

Leatherworking is also a thriving craft in Tunisia, with artisans in cities like Tunis and Sfax producing high-quality leather goods using traditional methods and materials. From hand-stitched bags and belts to intricately embossed wallets and sandals, Tunisian leatherworkers are renowned for their attention to detail and commitment to quality. Many artisans also incorporate traditional Tunisian motifs and designs into their work, creating pieces that are both stylish and culturally significant.

In addition to pottery, carpet weaving, and leatherworking, Tunisia is also known for its exquisite metalwork, wood carving, and embroidery. In the ancient city of Kairouan, for example, artisans create stunning brass and copper lamps, trays, and jewelry using techniques that have been passed down through generations. In the coastal town of Mahdia, skilled woodworkers carve intricate designs into furniture and decorative objects, while in the rural villages of the south, women embroider colorful textiles with traditional motifs and patterns.

Whether you're exploring the labyrinthine streets of the medina or visiting a rural artisan workshop, the craftsmanship of Tunisia is sure to leave a lasting impression. Each piece tells a story of tradition, skill, and cultural heritage, connecting the present with the past and preserving Tunisia's rich artisanal legacy for generations to come.

Music and Dance: Rhythms of Tunisian Culture

In the vibrant tapestry of Tunisian culture, music and dance play a central role, pulsating with the rhythms of tradition, history, and identity. From the lively beats of folk music to the graceful movements of traditional dances, Tunisian music and dance are expressions of the country's rich cultural heritage and diverse influences.

One of the most iconic forms of Tunisian music is known as Malouf, a classical Arab music genre that originated in Tunisia and is characterized by its intricate melodies and poetic lyrics. Malouf draws inspiration from classical Arabic poetry and Andalusian music, blending Arab, Berber, and Mediterranean influences into a harmonious fusion of sound. Accompanied by instruments such as the oud (a type of lute), violin, and flute, Malouf is often performed at weddings, festivals, and other special occasions, evoking a sense of nostalgia and cultural pride among Tunisians.

In addition to Malouf, Tunisia is also known for its vibrant folk music traditions, which vary from region to region and reflect the country's diverse cultural heritage. In the coastal regions, for example, you'll find lively sea shanties and fishing songs that celebrate the maritime lifestyle, while in the interior, the rhythms of the desert echo in the music of the Bedouin tribes, characterized by rhythmic drumming and chanting.

One of the most beloved Tunisian folk instruments is the bagpipe-like mezoued, which originated in North Africa and is commonly played at weddings, festivals, and other celebrations. The mezoued produces a distinctive, nasal sound that is instantly recognizable, and its infectious rhythms and melodies often inspire spontaneous dancing and merriment among listeners.

Speaking of dance, Tunisia boasts a rich tradition of folk and ceremonial dances, each with its own unique movements, costumes, and symbolism. One of the most famous Tunisian dances is the Stambali, a trance-like dance performed by members of the Gnawa community as part of spiritual rituals and healing ceremonies. Accompanied by rhythmic drumming and chanting, the Stambali is a powerful expression of faith, community, and cultural identity.

Another popular Tunisian dance is the Debka, a lively line dance that is often performed at weddings and other festive occasions. Originating in the Maghreb region, the Debka features synchronized footwork and hand movements that reflect the communal spirit and joyous celebration of Tunisian culture.

As you journey through Tunisia, you'll encounter a rich tapestry of music and dance that reflects the country's diverse cultural heritage and vibrant spirit. Whether you're tapping your feet to the infectious rhythms of a Malouf ensemble or joining in the joyous festivities of a traditional Debka dance, the music and dance of Tunisia are sure to leave a lasting impression on your heart and soul.

Festivals and Celebrations: Colorful Traditions and Religious Observances

In Tunisia, festivals and celebrations are a vibrant tapestry woven with colorful traditions, religious observances, and communal gatherings that reflect the country's rich cultural heritage and diverse influences. Throughout the year, Tunisians come together to mark significant events, honor religious traditions, and celebrate life's joys with music, dance, food, and fellowship.

One of the most widely celebrated festivals in Tunisia is Eid al-Fitr, which marks the end of Ramadan, the Islamic holy month of fasting. Eid al-Fitr is a joyous occasion characterized by prayers, feasting, and generosity, as families gather to share meals, exchange gifts, and give to those in need. Streets are adorned with colorful decorations, and children don new clothes as they join in the festivities, which often last for several days.

Another important religious observance in Tunisia is Eid al-Adha, also known as the Feast of Sacrifice, which commemorates Ibrahim's willingness to sacrifice his son Isma'il as an act of obedience to God. During Eid al-Adha, Muslims around the world slaughter livestock and distribute the meat to the less fortunate, symbolizing their willingness to make sacrifices for the sake of their faith. Families come together to share in the ritual slaughter, share meals, and strengthen bonds of kinship and community. In addition to religious festivals, Tunisia is also known for its vibrant cultural celebrations, which highlight the country's diverse cultural heritage and traditions. One such celebration is the Festival of the Sahara, held annually in the oasis town of Douz, where visitors gather to experience Bedouin culture, music, and traditions. The festival features camel races, traditional Bedouin weddings, and folk music and dance performances, offering a glimpse into the rich heritage of Tunisia's desert-dwelling tribes.

Another popular cultural event in Tunisia is the Carthage International Festival, held in the ancient city of Carthage, where visitors can enjoy a diverse array of performances, including music, theater, dance, and film. The festival attracts artists and performers from around the world, showcasing the cultural diversity and artistic talent of Tunisia and beyond.

Tunisia is also home to a number of regional festivals and celebrations, each with its own unique customs and traditions. In the coastal city of Sfax, for example, the annual International Olive Festival celebrates the country's olive harvest with parades, exhibitions, and tastings of local olive products. In the mountainous region of Zaghouan, the Festival of Roses pays tribute to the region's abundant rose fields with floral displays, beauty pageants, and cultural performances.

Whether it's a religious observance, a cultural celebration, or a regional festival, Tunisian festivals and celebrations are a testament to the country's rich cultural heritage, traditions, and spirit of community. From the bustling streets of Tunis to the remote villages of the interior, these colorful events bring people together, fostering a sense of unity, belonging, and pride in Tunisia's unique identity.

Tunisian Architecture: From Ancient Ruins to Modern Marvels

Tunisian architecture is a fascinating blend of ancient traditions, Islamic influences, and modern innovations, reflecting the country's rich history and diverse cultural heritage. From the ancient ruins of Carthage to the gleaming skyscrapers of Tunis, Tunisia's architectural landscape is a testament to its enduring legacy and evolving identity.

One of the most iconic examples of Tunisian architecture is the ancient city of Carthage, located just outside of Tunis. Founded by the Phoenicians in the 9th century BCE, Carthage was once a powerful trading empire and one of the largest cities in the ancient world. Today, visitors can explore the ruins of Carthage, including the impressive remnants of its grandiose buildings, such as the Baths of Antoninus and the Punic Ports.

In addition to Carthage, Tunisia is also home to a wealth of Roman and Byzantine ruins, including the impressive amphitheaters of El Jem and Dougga. These ancient structures are marvels of engineering and architecture, with their massive stone arches, intricate mosaics, and imposing facades offering a glimpse into Tunisia's rich architectural heritage.

Islamic architecture also plays a significant role in Tunisia's built environment, with mosques, madrasas, and palaces dotting the landscape. One of the most famous examples of Islamic architecture in Tunisia is the Great Mosque of Kairouan, considered one of the holiest sites in the Islamic world. Built in the 9th century, the Great Mosque is renowned for its stunning geometric patterns, ornate calligraphy, and towering minaret, which stands as a symbol of Tunisian identity and religious devotion.

In addition to traditional Islamic architecture, Tunisia is also home to a number of unique architectural styles influenced by its colonial past. During the French colonial period, which lasted from the late 19th century until the mid-20th century, French architects left their mark on Tunisia's cities, building grand boulevards, elegant villas, and public buildings in the neoclassical and Art Deco styles.

Today, Tunisia's architectural landscape continues to evolve, with modern skyscrapers, shopping malls, and residential complexes reshaping the skyline of cities like Tunis and Sousse. While these modern structures may seem worlds apart from the ancient ruins and traditional mosques that dot the countryside, they are a testament to Tunisia's ongoing commitment to progress, innovation, and economic development.

From the ancient ruins of Carthage to the soaring skyscrapers of Tunis, Tunisia's architectural heritage is a reflection of its rich history, diverse cultural influences, and unwavering spirit of innovation. Whether you're exploring ancient ruins, admiring traditional mosques, or marveling at modern marvels, Tunisia's architectural wonders are sure to leave a lasting impression on visitors from around the world.

Traditional Dress: Exploring Tunisian Clothing Styles

Traditional Tunisian dress is a vibrant reflection of the country's rich cultural heritage, blending influences from Arab, Berber, Mediterranean, and African traditions into unique and diverse clothing styles. From the flowing robes of the desert to the intricately embroidered garments of the coastal regions, Tunisian clothing tells a story of history, identity, and craftsmanship.

One of the most iconic pieces of traditional Tunisian clothing is the Jebba, a long, loose-fitting robe worn by both men and women. Made from lightweight fabric and typically adorned with elaborate embroidery along the neckline and sleeves, the Jebba is a symbol of elegance and sophistication. Men often pair the Jebba with a traditional woolen cloak called a Burnous, while women may accessorize with a colorful sash or headscarf.

For women, one of the most distinctive elements of traditional Tunisian dress is the Fouta, a rectangular piece of cloth that is wrapped around the body as a skirt or shawl. The Fouta is often made from colorful, patterned fabric and can be worn in a variety of ways, depending on the occasion and personal preference. In addition to the Fouta, women may also wear a traditional embroidered blouse called a Jebba Tounsi, which is typically adorned with intricate designs and motifs.

Another important element of traditional Tunisian dress is the Burnous, a hooded cloak made from wool or camel hair that is worn by men in rural areas, particularly in the mountainous regions of the interior. The Burnous provides protection from the harsh elements of the desert and serves as a symbol of status and identity among the nomadic tribes of Tunisia.

In addition to these traditional garments, Tunisian dress also incorporates a variety of accessories, including jewelry, belts, and footwear. Women often wear intricate silver jewelry, such as earrings, bracelets, and necklaces, as well as colorful beaded belts and sandals. Men may accessorize with leather belts, embroidered satchels, and handcrafted shoes.

One of the most famous examples of traditional Tunisian footwear is the Babouche, a soft leather slipper with a pointed toe and decorative stitching. Babouches are worn by both men and women and come in a variety of styles and colors, from simple, understated designs to elaborately embellished creations.

Overall, traditional Tunisian dress is a celebration of craftsmanship, culture, and heritage, with each garment and accessory telling a story of tradition, identity, and pride. Whether worn for special occasions or everyday wear, Tunisian clothing styles continue to inspire and captivate with their timeless elegance and enduring beauty.

Tunisian Literature: Voices of a Nation

Tunisian literature is a rich tapestry of voices that reflects the country's complex history, diverse cultural influences, and vibrant spirit of creativity. From ancient poetry and folk tales to contemporary novels and poetry collections, Tunisian writers have contributed to the global literary landscape with their unique perspectives, voices, and storytelling traditions.

One of the earliest forms of Tunisian literature is poetry, which has been an integral part of the country's cultural heritage for centuries. In the ancient city of Carthage, poets such as Hannibal and Virgil composed epic poems that celebrated the city's glory and explored themes of love, war, and destiny. Over the centuries, poetry continued to flourish in Tunisia, with poets like Ibn Khaldun and Ibn Arabi writing influential works that shaped Islamic thought and philosophy.

In addition to poetry, Tunisian literature is also rich in folk tales and oral traditions, which have been passed down through generations and continue to inspire writers and storytellers today. These tales often feature themes of adventure, magic, and morality, and are filled with colorful characters, mythical creatures, and fantastical settings. One of the most famous Tunisian folk tales is "The Story of Antar and Abla," an epic romance that has been told and retold for centuries, inspiring countless works of literature, music, and art.

During the colonial period, Tunisian literature underwent a period of transformation and resistance, as writers and intellectuals used their creative talents to challenge colonial rule and assert Tunisian identity. Writers such as Tahar Haddad and Mohamed Salah Ben Mrad penned essays, novels, and poetry that explored themes of national liberation, social justice, and cultural revival, laying the foundation for Tunisia's independence movement.

In the years following independence in 1956, Tunisian literature experienced a renaissance, with writers and poets exploring new forms of expression and addressing pressing social and political issues facing the country. One of the most prominent figures of this period was Albert Memmi, whose novels such as "The Pillar of Salt" and "The Colonizer and the Colonized" explored themes of identity, alienation, and post-colonialism.

Today, Tunisian literature continues to thrive, with a new generation of writers and poets emerging to explore the complexities of contemporary Tunisian society and culture. Writers such as Amina Saïd, Shukri Mabkhout, and Anis Chouchene are gaining international recognition for their thought-provoking novels, short stories, and poetry collections that tackle issues such as identity, migration, and social change.

Whether it's ancient poetry, folk tales, colonial resistance literature, or contemporary novels, Tunisian literature offers a diverse and compelling array of voices that capture the essence of the nation and its people. Through their words and stories, Tunisian writers continue to inspire, enlighten, and challenge readers around the world, ensuring that the rich literary tradition of Tunisia will endure for generations to come.

Tunisian Cinema: A Growing Industry

Tunisian cinema is a dynamic and evolving industry that has gained international recognition for its diverse storytelling, innovative filmmaking techniques, and unique cultural perspective. From its early beginnings in the 1920s to its burgeoning success in the 21st century, Tunisian cinema has played a significant role in shaping the country's cultural identity and global reputation.

The history of Tunisian cinema dates back to the early 20th century, with the establishment of the first film production companies in the 1920s. One of the pioneers of Tunisian cinema was Albert Samama-Chikli, who produced the country's first silent film, "The Child of the Sun," in 1923. Over the following decades, Tunisian filmmakers continued to produce a diverse range of films, including documentaries, short films, and feature-length dramas, often exploring themes of national identity, social justice, and cultural heritage.

One of the most significant developments in Tunisian cinema occurred in the 1960s and 1970s, with the emergence of the "Tunisian New Wave," a movement characterized by its experimental storytelling, artistic innovation, and political engagement. Filmmakers such as Nacer Khemir, Férid Boughedir, and Moufida Tlatli gained international acclaim for their bold and provocative films, which challenged conventions and pushed the boundaries of Tunisian cinema.

In 1987, Tunisian cinema received a major boost with the establishment of the National Cinema Center (CNC), a government agency tasked with supporting and promoting the development of Tunisian film industry. The CNC provided funding, training, and resources to aspiring filmmakers, enabling them to produce high-quality films that reflected the diversity and complexity of Tunisian society.

In recent years, Tunisian cinema has experienced a renaissance, with a new generation of filmmakers emerging to tell their stories and share their unique perspectives with the world. Directors such as Kaouther Ben Hania, Leyla Bouzid, and Mohamed Ben Attia have gained international recognition for their critically acclaimed films, which have won awards at prestigious film festivals around the world.

One of the most notable achievements in Tunisian cinema in recent years was the success of the film "Hedi," directed by Mohamed Ben Attia, which won the Best First Feature award at the 2016 Berlin International Film Festival. The film received widespread acclaim for its poignant storytelling, authentic performances, and sensitive portrayal of contemporary Tunisian life.

In addition to narrative films, Tunisian cinema also encompasses a wide range of genres and styles, including documentaries, animation, and experimental cinema. Filmmakers continue to explore new techniques and storytelling methods, pushing the boundaries of what is possible in Tunisian cinema and attracting audiences both at home and abroad.

Overall, Tunisian cinema is a vibrant and growing industry that continues to evolve and thrive, fueled by the creativity, talent, and passion of its filmmakers. With its rich cultural heritage, diverse storytelling traditions, and commitment to artistic excellence, Tunisian cinema is poised to make an even greater impact on the global stage in the years to come.

Language and Dialects: Understanding Tunisian Arabic and French

Language and dialects in Tunisia reflect the country's complex history and cultural diversity. Tunisian Arabic is the most widely spoken language, serving as the primary means of communication for the majority of the population. Tunisian Arabic, also known as Derja, is a distinct dialect of Arabic that has been influenced by Berber, French, and other languages over the centuries. It is characterized by its unique vocabulary, grammar, and pronunciation, which set it apart from other varieties of Arabic spoken in the region.

One of the defining features of Tunisian Arabic is its use of loanwords from French, Italian, and Berber, reflecting the country's history of colonialism, trade, and cultural exchange. French, in particular, has had a significant impact on Tunisian Arabic, with many words and phrases borrowed from French and integrated into everyday speech. This linguistic fusion gives Tunisian Arabic its distinctive flavor and reflects the country's multicultural heritage.

In addition to Tunisian Arabic, French is also widely spoken and understood in Tunisia, serving as the second language of education, government, and business. French was introduced to Tunisia during the colonial period and has remained an important language in the country ever since. Today, French is taught in schools and universities across Tunisia, and many Tunisians are fluent in both French and Arabic, using each language in different contexts depending on the situation.

While Tunisian Arabic and French are the two primary languages spoken in Tunisia, the country is also home to a number of other languages and dialects, including Berber, Italian, and English. Berber languages, such as Tamazight, are spoken by the Berber ethnic minority in Tunisia and have been recognized as official languages alongside Arabic since the adoption of the country's new constitution in 2014.

Overall, language and dialects play a central role in Tunisian identity and culture, reflecting the country's diverse heritage and complex social dynamics. Whether speaking Tunisian Arabic with friends and family, conducting business in French, or preserving traditional Berber languages, Tunisians embrace linguistic diversity as a source of strength and pride. Through language, Tunisians express their cultural identity, share their stories, and connect with one another, forging bonds that transcend linguistic differences and unite them as a nation.

The Influence of Berber Languages: Tracing Tunisia's Linguistic Heritage

The influence of Berber languages on Tunisia's linguistic heritage is profound and far-reaching, shaping the country's identity and cultural landscape in significant ways. Berber languages, also known as Tamazight languages, have been spoken in North Africa for thousands of years, predating the arrival of Arabic and other languages in the region. In Tunisia, Berber languages have played a crucial role in shaping the linguistic diversity and cultural richness of the country.

The Berber languages spoken in Tunisia belong to the Afro-Asiatic language family, which includes several distinct dialects and varieties. These languages are primarily spoken by the Berber ethnic minority, who have inhabited North Africa for millennia and have preserved their unique cultural traditions and languages despite centuries of cultural and linguistic assimilation.

One of the most significant Berber languages spoken in Tunisia is Tamazight, which is widely spoken by the Berber communities in the mountainous regions of the interior. Tamazight is a complex and diverse language with multiple dialects and variations, each with its own unique vocabulary, grammar, and pronunciation. Despite centuries of Arabization and colonialism, Tamazight has endured as a symbol of Berber identity and resistance, with efforts underway to preserve and promote the language through education, media, and cultural initiatives.

In addition to Tamazight, other Berber languages spoken in Tunisia include Tumzabt, Chaouia, and Ghadamesi, each of which has its own distinct linguistic characteristics and cultural significance. These languages are primarily spoken in rural areas and small communities, where Berber cultural traditions remain strong and vibrant.

The influence of Berber languages on Tunisian Arabic is evident in the vocabulary, grammar, and pronunciation of the dialects spoken throughout the country. Many words and phrases in Tunisian Arabic are derived from Berber languages, reflecting the close historical and cultural ties between the Berber and Arab communities in Tunisia.

In recent years, there has been a renewed interest in promoting and preserving Berber languages in Tunisia, with initiatives aimed at increasing awareness, education, and literacy in Tamazight and other Berber dialects. These efforts are part of a broader movement to celebrate Tunisia's linguistic diversity and ensure that Berber languages continue to thrive for generations to come.

Overall, the influence of Berber languages on Tunisia's linguistic heritage is a testament to the country's rich and diverse cultural tapestry. From the mountains of the interior to the bustling cities along the coast, Berber languages have left an indelible mark on Tunisia's identity, shaping the way its people speak, think, and interact with the world around them.

Education in Tunisia: Past, Present, and Future

Education in Tunisia has undergone significant transformations over the years, reflecting the country's commitment to providing quality education for its citizens and shaping the future of its society. From its early beginnings in ancient times to its modern-day educational system, Tunisia has prioritized education as a cornerstone of its development and progress.

Historically, education in Tunisia dates back to ancient times when scholars and philosophers in Carthage and other ancient cities imparted knowledge to the elite classes. However, it wasn't until the Islamic Golden Age that formal educational institutions, known as madrasas, were established, providing education in subjects such as theology, law, and science.

During the colonial period, Tunisia's education system underwent significant changes as French authorities introduced modern educational reforms aimed at assimilating Tunisian youth into French culture and language. French became the language of instruction in schools, and Western-style educational institutions were established, including the University of Ez-Zitouna, which was founded in 737 AD and remains one of the oldest universities in the world.

Following independence in 1956, Tunisia embarked on a comprehensive program of educational reform aimed at expanding access to education and modernizing the curriculum. The government invested heavily in building schools, training teachers, and expanding educational opportunities for all Tunisian citizens, regardless of their socioeconomic background.

Today, Tunisia's education system is characterized by its emphasis on universal access to education, free and compulsory education for children ages 6 to 16, and a commitment to providing quality education for all. The system is divided into three main stages: primary education, which lasts for six years; secondary education, which consists of three cycles and lasts for seven years; and higher education, which includes universities, institutes, and vocational training centers.

Primary education in Tunisia focuses on basic literacy and numeracy skills, as well as subjects such as Arabic, French, mathematics, science, and social studies. Secondary education builds on these foundations and offers students the opportunity to specialize in academic or vocational tracks, depending on their interests and career aspirations.

Tunisia's higher education system is highly regarded in the region and offers a wide range of academic programs and research opportunities across various disciplines. The country's universities, including the University of Tunis and the University of Sousse, attract students from across the Arab world and beyond, contributing to Tunisia's reputation as a center of learning and innovation.

Looking to the future, Tunisia faces challenges in ensuring equitable access to education, improving the quality of teaching and learning, and aligning education with the needs of the modern economy. However, with continued investment in education, a commitment to innovation and reform, and a focus on empowering the next generation of Tunisian leaders, the future of education in Tunisia looks bright.

Religion and Society: Islam in Tunisian Life

Religion, particularly Islam, plays a central role in Tunisian society, shaping both individual lives and the broader cultural landscape. As a predominantly Muslim country, Tunisia's social fabric is deeply intertwined with Islamic beliefs, traditions, and practices. Islam was introduced to Tunisia in the 7th century AD with the Arab conquests, and it quickly became the dominant religion, replacing Christianity and indigenous faiths.

One of the key aspects of Islam in Tunisian life is the practice of the five pillars of Islam: Shahada (the declaration of faith), Salat (prayer), Zakat (almsgiving), Sawm (fasting during the month of Ramadan), and Hajj (pilgrimage to Mecca). These pillars serve as the foundation of Islamic faith and guide the daily lives of Tunisian Muslims, influencing everything from personal conduct to social interactions.

In Tunisia, Islam is not just a set of religious beliefs, but also a cultural and social identity that shapes many aspects of daily life. From the call to prayer echoing from minarets to the observance of religious holidays such as Eid al-Fitr and Eid al-Adha, Islam is deeply ingrained in the rhythm of Tunisian life. Tunisian society places a high value on piety, humility, and community solidarity, all of which are central tenets of Islamic teachings.

Despite its predominantly Muslim population, Tunisia is known for its relatively moderate and tolerant interpretation of Islam. The country has a long tradition of religious diversity and coexistence, with Muslims living alongside small communities of Christians, Jews, and other religious minorities. The Tunisian government has historically promoted a secularist approach to governance, emphasizing the separation of religion and state and guaranteeing freedom of religion for all citizens.

In recent years, however, Tunisia has experienced a resurgence of Islamic conservatism and religious activism, fueled in part by political instability, economic challenges, and social inequalities. The rise of political Islam has led to debates and tensions over the role of religion in public life, with some advocating for a greater influence of Islamic law (Sharia) in the legal system and others calling for a more secular and pluralistic society.

Despite these challenges, Tunisia remains a vibrant and diverse society where Islam continues to play a central role in shaping individual and collective identities. Whether through daily prayers, religious rituals, or acts of charity and compassion, Islam remains a cornerstone of Tunisian life, providing comfort, guidance, and a sense of belonging to millions of Tunisians across the country.

Women's Rights in Tunisia: Progress and Challenges

Women's rights in Tunisia have seen significant progress over the years, making the country a pioneer in the Arab world in terms of gender equality. Since gaining independence in 1956, Tunisia has implemented various legal reforms and social policies aimed at promoting women's rights and empowering women in all aspects of society.

One of the most notable milestones in Tunisia's journey toward gender equality was the adoption of the Code of Personal Status in 1956. This landmark legislation, often hailed as one of the most progressive family laws in the Arab world, granted women equal rights in areas such as marriage, divorce, and inheritance. It abolished polygamy, established a minimum age for marriage, and gave women the right to seek divorce on equal terms with men.

The Code of Personal Status also introduced measures to promote women's education and employment opportunities, encouraging women to pursue higher education and enter the workforce. As a result, Tunisian women today have higher levels of education and participation in the labor force compared to many other countries in the region.

In addition to legal reforms, Tunisia has also made strides in promoting women's political participation and representation. In 2011, following the ousting of

President Zine El Abidine Ben Ali during the Arab Spring uprising, Tunisia adopted a new constitution that enshrined gender equality and guaranteed women's rights as fundamental principles of the state. The constitution mandates that women must hold at least 50% of the seats in elected assemblies, ensuring women's voices are heard in the political decision-making process.

Despite these achievements, women in Tunisia still face challenges and inequalities, particularly in areas such as gender-based violence, economic empowerment, and reproductive rights. Domestic violence remains a pervasive issue, with many women experiencing physical, psychological, and sexual abuse in their homes. Although laws against domestic violence exist, implementation and enforcement remain inadequate, leaving many women vulnerable to abuse.

Economic empowerment is another area where women in Tunisia continue to face barriers. While women have made significant strides in education and workforce participation, they still encounter gender discrimination in hiring practices, wage disparities, and access to economic opportunities. Many women, especially those in rural areas and marginalized communities, struggle to access resources and support to start businesses or pursue entrepreneurship.

Reproductive rights are also a contentious issue in Tunisia, with debates over issues such as abortion, contraception, and reproductive health services.

While Tunisia has relatively liberal laws regarding abortion compared to other Arab countries, access to safe and legal abortion services remains limited, and women who seek abortions often face stigma and discrimination.

Despite these challenges, Tunisia remains committed to advancing women's rights and gender equality through legislative reforms, public awareness campaigns, and international partnerships. With ongoing efforts to address gender-based violence, promote economic empowerment, and protect reproductive rights, Tunisia is poised to continue its journey toward achieving full equality and empowerment for all women.

Sports and Recreation: From Football to Camel Racing

Sports and recreation hold a significant place in Tunisian society, offering a diverse range of activities that cater to people of all ages and interests. Football, or soccer as it's known in the United States, is undoubtedly the most popular sport in Tunisia and enjoys widespread participation and fervent support from fans across the country. The Tunisian national football team, known as "The Eagles of Carthage," has achieved notable success on the international stage, including qualifying for multiple FIFA World Cup tournaments and winning the Africa Cup of Nations in 2004.

Beyond football, Tunisia boasts a rich tradition of athletics, with track and field, basketball, volleyball, and handball among the most popular sports. Tunisian athletes have excelled in various disciplines, earning medals and accolades in regional and international competitions. Notably, Habiba Ghribi made history as the first Tunisian woman to win an Olympic medal in athletics, securing silver in the 3000-meter steeplechase at the 2012 London Olympics.

In addition to mainstream sports, Tunisia offers unique recreational activities that reflect its cultural heritage and natural landscapes. Camel racing, for example, is a traditional sport enjoyed primarily in rural areas and desert regions, where camel breeders and enthusiasts gather to showcase their animals' speed and agility. The annual Tozeur International Festival of the Sahara features camel races among its many attractions, attracting spectators and participants from around the world.

Water sports are also popular in Tunisia, thanks to its extensive coastline along the Mediterranean Sea. From swimming and snorkeling to windsurfing and kiteboarding, there are plenty of opportunities for aquatic adventures along Tunisia's sandy beaches and crystal-clear waters. The island of Djerba, in particular, is renowned for its water sports facilities and attracts enthusiasts from far and wide.

Tennis has also gained popularity in Tunisia, with several professional tournaments held annually, including the Tunis Open, which is part of the ATP Challenger Tour. The country has produced talented tennis players who have achieved success on the international circuit, contributing to Tunisia's growing reputation as a hub for tennis in North Africa.

Beyond organized sports, Tunisians also enjoy a variety of recreational activities, such as hiking, camping, and picnicking in the country's national parks and nature reserves. The Atlas Mountains in the north and the Sahara Desert in the south offer breathtaking landscapes and opportunities for outdoor adventure, attracting nature lovers and thrill-seekers alike.

Overall, sports and recreation play a vital role in Tunisian culture, providing opportunities for physical activity, social interaction, and cultural expression. Whether cheering on their favorite football team, riding camels across the desert, or exploring the country's natural wonders, Tunisians find joy and fulfillment in the diverse array of sports and leisure activities available to them.

Economy and Trade: Navigating Tunisia's Business Landscape

The economy of Tunisia is characterized by a diverse range of industries and sectors, reflecting the country's strategic location, natural resources, and skilled workforce. Historically, Tunisia has relied on agriculture as a primary source of income, with olive oil, citrus fruits, and dates among its main exports. However, in recent decades, the economy has undergone significant diversification, with manufacturing, services, and tourism emerging as key drivers of growth and development.

Manufacturing plays a crucial role in Tunisia's economy, accounting for a significant portion of the country's GDP and employing a large segment of the workforce. The manufacturing sector encompasses a wide range of industries, including textiles, automotive, electronics, and aerospace. Tunisia has positioned itself as a leading exporter of textiles and clothing, thanks to its skilled labor force, competitive production costs, and preferential trade agreements with the European Union and other international markets.

The automotive industry is another important sector of Tunisia's economy, with several multinational companies, including Renault and Peugeot, establishing manufacturing plants in the country. These plants produce a variety of vehicles for domestic consumption and export, contributing to

Tunisia's reputation as a regional hub for automotive production.

In addition to manufacturing, the services sector plays a significant role in Tunisia's economy, accounting for a growing share of GDP and employment. The services sector encompasses a wide range of activities, including banking and finance, telecommunications, tourism, and information technology. Tunisia's strategic location and well-developed infrastructure have positioned it as an attractive destination for foreign investment in services, particularly in the areas of business process outsourcing, call centers, and software development.

Tourism is a vital sector of Tunisia's economy, contributing to foreign exchange earnings, job creation, and regional development. The country's rich history, cultural heritage, and diverse landscapes, including sandy beaches, ancient ruins, and bustling markets, attract millions of visitors each year. However, the tourism industry has faced challenges in recent years due to security concerns and political instability, leading to a decline in tourist arrivals and revenue.

Trade plays a crucial role in Tunisia's economy, with the country actively participating in regional and international trade agreements to facilitate the flow of goods and services. Tunisia is a member of several trade blocs, including the Arab Maghreb Union, the Greater Arab Free Trade Area, and the Agadir Agreement, which promote economic integration and cooperation among member states.

Despite its economic potential, Tunisia faces challenges in promoting sustainable and inclusive growth, including high unemployment rates, income inequality, and structural weaknesses in the economy. The government has implemented various reforms and initiatives to address these challenges, including investment in education and training, infrastructure development, and support for small and medium-sized enterprises.

Overall, Tunisia's economy offers opportunities for growth and investment across multiple sectors, driven by a skilled workforce, strategic location, and commitment to economic reform and modernization. With continued investment in key industries and efforts to address structural challenges, Tunisia is well-positioned to navigate its business landscape and achieve sustainable development in the years to come.

Tourism in Tunisia: Exploring the Country's Most Iconic Sites

Tourism in Tunisia is a vibrant and diverse industry, attracting visitors from around the world to explore the country's rich history, stunning landscapes, and vibrant culture. From ancient ruins to sandy beaches, Tunisia offers a wealth of attractions that appeal to travelers of all interests and preferences.

One of the most iconic sites in Tunisia is the ancient city of Carthage, located just outside of the capital city, Tunis. Carthage was once a powerful Phoenician city-state and later became the capital of the Carthaginian Empire, one of the greatest civilizations of the ancient Mediterranean world. Today, visitors to Carthage can explore the ruins of ancient temples, theaters, and residential quarters, offering a fascinating glimpse into the city's storied past.

Another must-visit destination in Tunisia is the UNESCO World Heritage site of Dougga, often referred to as the "best-preserved Roman city in North Africa." Situated in the hills of northern Tunisia, Dougga boasts well-preserved Roman ruins, including a theater, temples, and a forum, providing visitors with an immersive experience of life in ancient times.

For those seeking relaxation and sun-soaked beaches, the coastal town of Hammamet is a popular destination. Known for its white sandy beaches and crystal-clear waters, Hammamet offers a range of water sports activities, luxurious resorts, and vibrant nightlife options. Nearby, the resort island of Djerba beckons with its palm-fringed beaches, ancient villages, and colorful markets.

Inland, the city of Kairouan holds great significance as one of the holiest cities in Islam and is home to the Great Mosque of Kairouan, one of the oldest and most important mosques in the Islamic world. Visitors can explore the city's historic medina, browse its bustling souks, and admire its architectural treasures, including ornate palaces and ancient city gates.

No visit to Tunisia would be complete without experiencing the stunning landscapes of the Sahara Desert. The town of Tozeur serves as a gateway to the desert, offering camel treks, desert safaris, and visits to traditional Berber villages. Travelers can marvel at the towering sand dunes, explore ancient ksour (fortified villages), and spend nights under the starry desert sky.

Throughout Tunisia, visitors can immerse themselves in the country's rich cultural heritage through festivals, music, and cuisine. From the annual Carthage International Festival, which showcases performances by artists from around the world, to the lively street markets where locals and visitors alike can sample traditional Tunisian dishes such as couscous, brik, and tagine, Tunisia offers a feast for the senses at every turn.

With its diverse array of attractions, warm hospitality, and rich cultural tapestry, Tunisia remains a captivating destination for travelers seeking adventure, history, and relaxation in equal measure. Whether exploring ancient ruins, basking on sandy beaches, or venturing into the heart of the Sahara, visitors to Tunisia are sure to be enchanted by the country's timeless beauty and enduring charm.

Medinas and Souks: Shopping and Sightseeing in Tunisia's Old Towns

In Tunisia, the medinas and souks are the beating heart of the country's old towns, offering a vibrant tapestry of history, culture, and commerce. These ancient marketplaces have been bustling hubs of activity for centuries, serving as centers of trade, social gatherings, and artistic expression.

One of the most famous medinas in Tunisia is found in the capital city of Tunis. The Medina of Tunis, a UNESCO World Heritage site, is a labyrinthine maze of narrow alleyways, hidden courtyards, and historic monuments. Visitors can wander through the bustling streets, marvel at the intricate architecture of centuries-old buildings, and discover hidden gems tucked away in every corner.

Within the Medina of Tunis, the souks offer a treasure trove of goods, from handcrafted textiles and leather goods to spices, ceramics, and jewelry. The souks are a paradise for shoppers, with vendors calling out to passersby, inviting them to browse their wares and haggle over prices. Bargaining is a time-honored tradition in Tunisian souks, and visitors can test their negotiating skills while hunting for unique souvenirs and gifts to take home.

Beyond Tunis, other cities in Tunisia boast their own vibrant medinas and souks, each with its own distinct character and charm. In Sousse, the Medina of Sousse is a bustling marketplace where visitors can explore ancient ramparts, browse colorful stalls, and sample local delicacies such as freshly baked pastries and aromatic spices.

The Medina of Sfax, another UNESCO World Heritage site, offers a glimpse into Tunisia's maritime history, with its winding streets lined with merchants selling everything from fish and seafood to textiles and handicrafts. The city's iconic clock tower, known as the Kasbah Mosque, stands as a symbol of Sfax's rich cultural heritage and architectural prowess.

In Kairouan, the Medina of Kairouan is a testament to the city's status as a center of Islamic learning and spirituality. Here, visitors can wander through narrow alleys flanked by whitewashed houses, visit historic mosques and madrasas, and shop for traditional handicrafts such as carpets, pottery, and brassware.

Throughout Tunisia, the medinas and souks offer more than just shopping opportunities—they are living museums where visitors can immerse themselves in the sights, sounds, and smells of everyday life in Tunisia. Whether exploring ancient alleyways, sampling local cuisine, or bargaining for treasures, a visit to Tunisia's medinas and souks is an unforgettable journey back in time.

Beach Resorts: Sun, Sand, and Relaxation on Tunisia's Coastline

When it comes to beach resorts, Tunisia offers an enticing blend of sun, sand, and relaxation along its picturesque coastline. Stretching for miles along the Mediterranean Sea, Tunisia's beaches are renowned for their golden sands, crystal-clear waters, and year-round sunshine, making them an ideal destination for beach lovers and sun seekers alike.

One of the most popular beach destinations in Tunisia is Hammamet, known as the "Tunisian Saint-Tropez." Located just a short drive from the capital city of Tunis, Hammamet boasts a stunning coastline dotted with luxurious resorts, boutique hotels, and private villas. Visitors to Hammamet can relax on pristine beaches, swim in the warm waters of the Mediterranean, and enjoy a wide range of water sports activities, including jet skiing, parasailing, and banana boating.

Further south along the coast lies the resort town of Sousse, renowned for its historic medina and beautiful beaches. Sousse's sandy shores are perfect for sunbathing and swimming, while its lively waterfront promenade offers a variety of cafes, restaurants, and bars where visitors can unwind and enjoy stunning views of the sea.

Nearby, the island of Djerba beckons with its palm-fringed beaches and laid-back atmosphere. Djerba is home to some of Tunisia's most luxurious beach resorts, offering world-class amenities, fine dining, and unparalleled service. Visitors to Djerba can explore ancient villages, visit historic mosques and synagogues, or simply relax on the beach and soak up the island's tranquil ambiance.

For those seeking a more secluded beach experience, the resort town of Tabarka is an ideal choice. Tucked away on Tunisia's northwest coast, Tabarka is known for its rugged coastline, rocky coves, and pristine beaches. The town's clear blue waters are perfect for snorkeling and diving, with colorful coral reefs and marine life waiting to be discovered beneath the surface.

In addition to its natural beauty, Tunisia's beach resorts offer a wide range of amenities and activities to suit every traveler's preferences. From luxurious spa treatments and championship golf courses to cultural excursions and culinary experiences, there is no shortage of ways to relax and unwind along Tunisia's stunning coastline.

Whether seeking adventure or relaxation, Tunisia's beach resorts provide the perfect backdrop for an unforgettable vacation experience. With their idyllic settings, warm hospitality, and endless opportunities for fun and relaxation, Tunisia's beaches are sure to leave a lasting impression on visitors from around the world.

Adventure Tourism: Exploring Tunisia's Natural Wonders

Adventure tourism in Tunisia offers a thrilling journey into the heart of the country's natural wonders, from rugged mountains to vast deserts and everything in between. With its diverse landscapes and rich biodiversity, Tunisia provides ample opportunities for outdoor enthusiasts to embark on unforgettable adventures.

One of the most iconic natural attractions in Tunisia is the Sahara Desert, the largest hot desert in the world. Travelers can explore the desert on camel treks, 4x4 excursions, or even on foot, immersing themselves in the breathtaking scenery of towering sand dunes, expansive salt flats, and ancient oases. Camping under the starry desert sky is a highlight for many, offering a chance to experience the silence and solitude of the desert night.

In the north of the country, the Atlas Mountains offer a playground for adventure seekers, with opportunities for hiking, mountain biking, and rock climbing. Jebel Chambi, the highest peak in Tunisia, beckons climbers to conquer its summit and enjoy panoramic views of the surrounding landscape. The mountainous region is also home to lush forests, picturesque valleys, and cascading waterfalls, providing a refreshing escape from the desert heat.

Tunisia's coastline is another playground for adventure tourism, with opportunities for snorkeling, scuba diving, and sea kayaking. The crystal-clear waters of the Mediterranean Sea are teeming with marine life, including colorful coral reefs, tropical fish, and even the occasional dolphin or sea turtle. Diving enthusiasts can explore underwater caves, shipwrecks, and coral gardens, while kayakers can paddle along scenic coastlines and hidden coves.

For adrenaline junkies, Tunisia offers opportunities for paragliding, skydiving, and hot air ballooning, providing a bird's-eye view of the country's stunning landscapes. The coastal town of Cap Bon is a popular spot for paragliding, with its favorable winds and panoramic views of the sea and countryside.

In addition to its natural beauty, Tunisia's adventure tourism industry is supported by a network of experienced guides, tour operators, and outdoor outfitters who ensure the safety and enjoyment of travelers. Whether exploring the desert, scaling mountains, or diving beneath the waves, adventure seekers in Tunisia are sure to find an experience that ignites their sense of wonder and leaves them with memories to last a lifetime.

Sustainable Development: Preserving Tunisia's Heritage for Future Generations

Sustainable development in Tunisia is a vital endeavor aimed at preserving the country's rich cultural heritage and natural resources for future generations. As Tunisia continues to develop and grow, there is a growing recognition of the importance of balancing economic progress with environmental conservation and social equity.

One area where sustainable development is particularly important is in preserving Tunisia's cultural heritage. The country is home to a wealth of archaeological sites, historic monuments, and traditional communities that are integral to its identity and tourism industry. Efforts to protect and conserve these cultural assets include initiatives to restore ancient ruins, promote heritage tourism, and support local artisans and craftsmen.

Environmental sustainability is also a key focus of Tunisia's development strategy. The country is taking steps to address environmental challenges such as deforestation, soil erosion, and water scarcity through measures such as reforestation programs, sustainable land management practices, and water conservation efforts. Additionally, Tunisia is investing in renewable energy sources such as solar and wind power to reduce its reliance on fossil fuels and combat climate change.

In the tourism sector, sustainable development practices are being implemented to minimize the impact of tourism on the environment and local communities. This includes promoting eco-friendly accommodations, encouraging responsible tourism practices, and supporting community-based tourism initiatives that empower local residents and preserve cultural traditions.

Furthermore, Tunisia is working to promote social equity and inclusivity as part of its sustainable development agenda. Initiatives to improve access to education, healthcare, and employment opportunities are underway, particularly in rural and marginalized areas. Additionally, efforts to empower women and youth, promote gender equality, and support minority groups are essential for creating a more just and equitable society.

Overall, sustainable development in Tunisia is a multifaceted endeavor that requires collaboration between government agencies, civil society organizations, the private sector, and local communities. By adopting holistic approaches that balance economic growth with environmental protection and social equity, Tunisia can ensure that its heritage is preserved, its natural resources are safeguarded, and its people thrive now and in the future.

Epilogue

In this journey through Tunisia, we've delved deep into the heart of this North African gem, uncovering its rich history, vibrant culture, stunning landscapes, and warm hospitality. From the ancient ruins of Carthage to the bustling streets of Tunis, from the golden beaches of Hammamet to the majestic Sahara Desert, Tunisia has captivated us with its beauty and diversity.

We've traced the footsteps of civilizations past, from the Phoenicians and Romans to the Arabs and Ottomans, witnessing the rise and fall of empires and the enduring legacy they've left behind. We've marveled at the architectural wonders of ancient cities like Carthage, Dougga, and Kairouan, and explored the labyrinthine medinas and souks that pulse with life in towns and cities across the country.

We've savored the flavors of Tunisian cuisine, from fragrant couscous and spicy harissa to flaky brik and sweet makroudh, experiencing the unique blend of Mediterranean, Arab, and Berber influences that define the country's culinary identity. We've reveled in the rhythms of Tunisian music and dance, from the haunting melodies of the oud to the energetic beats of the darbuka, celebrating the rich tapestry of cultural expression that permeates every aspect of life in Tunisia.

We've learned about the challenges and triumphs of Tunisia's journey to independence, from its struggles against colonialism to its ongoing efforts to build a democratic society that respects human rights and fosters economic development. We've explored the role of religion, education, and women's rights in shaping Tunisian society, gaining insights into the complex interplay of tradition and modernity that defines the country's social fabric.

As we reflect on our journey through Tunisia, we are reminded of the resilience and spirit of its people, who have overcome adversity with grace and determination. We are inspired by the natural beauty of its landscapes, the richness of its heritage, and the warmth of its hospitality. And we are hopeful for the future of this extraordinary country, as it continues to chart its course on the path of progress and prosperity.

In closing, Tunisia stands as a shining example of resilience, diversity, and hope in a world filled with challenges and uncertainties. As we bid farewell to this captivating land, may its story serve as a reminder of the power of human spirit to overcome adversity and create a brighter future for generations to come.

Printed in Great Britain
by Amazon